STRENGTHS

BASED

SELLING

BASED ON DECADES OF GALLUP'S RESEARCH INTO
HIGH-PERFORMING SALESPEOPLE

TONY RUTIGLIANO AND BRIAN BRIM

GALLUP PRESS
1251 Avenue of the Americas
23rd Floor
New York, NY 10020

Library of Congress Control Number: 2010936741
ISBN: 978-1-59562-048-4

First Printing: 2010
10 9 8 7 6 5 4 3 2 1

My former colleagues at ADP are some of the finest sales executives and developers of sales talent I've ever known. Most of all, thanks to the busiest and most extraordinary person I know, my wife Karen, who gives me support and smiles, despite my all too many airline miles.

Tony Rutigliano

To my wonderful wife Kim and our amazing daughters Chloe and Jerri, who together create a place of warmth and love to always come home to. And to my dad (who while alive was a trusted salesperson to many) and my mom, who have always believed in my strengths.

Brian Brim

Each of the people listed below was interviewed extensively as part of the research for this book. They have all been highly successful in sales roles during their careers and were recommended by their organizations as strong representatives of the sales profession. We want to thank them personally for providing their time, talent, and insights and for being an important part of *Strengths Based Selling*. Though all are not quoted directly, in all cases, their ideas influenced the book. We hope you will learn, as we did, a great deal from their stories and expertise.

- Mike Astrauskas, Sales Representative, Cargill

- Ron Barczak, Knoxville Area Sales Representative, Stryker Surgical

- TC Crafts, Assistant Centre Director/Program Director, Jenny Craig

- Dana Fiser, Vice President, Corporate Operations, Jenny Craig

- Kelly Matthews, Account Manager, Mars Snackfood

- Geoff Nyheim, Vice President, Microsoft Online Services

- Laura Richardson, Consultant, Jenny Craig

- Rita Robison, Senior Vice President, Jones Lang LaSalle

- Steve Sieck, Sales Director — Oncology North, Pfizer

- Dirk Tinley, Mortgage Loan Officer, U.S. Bank Home Mortgage

- Alain Tremblay, Senior Manager, Business Development, Standard Life

- John Wells, Senior Vice President for Americas Floorcoverings, Interface

- Pfizer Oncology focus group on team selling. Special thanks to District Business Manager Mike Scouvart for giving us access to his team: Kelly Beeman, Gary Dille, Jim Dymski, Ben Holtvogt, Robert Louwers, Rose Peluso-Mroz, Andrea Ochall, Bradley Salmon, Peter Steffan, Mel Walker-Poultan, and Brian Wright

TABLE OF CONTENTS

Those who follow the part of themselves that is great will become great. Those who follow the part that is small will become small.

— *Meng Tzu*

Two Myths About Sales

THIS CHAPTER'S KEY POINTS

- Great salespeople are fairly rare, but if you're one of them, good. Don't let anyone tell you that you're just part of a crowd.

- There is no one right way to sell. You'll get the best results by building on who you already are.

Jerry walks into a room full of strangers and feels excited. To him, this is a little slice of heaven. It's his opportunity to make 20 new connections with 20 potential prospects. He gets energy from these situations. By the end of the evening, he feels even more energized, and so do his 20 new contacts.

Melinda looks at the table of numbers in front of her, and she immediately begins to see a story in the data. She loves that feeling. She gets a sense of accomplishment whenever the stories in the numbers emerge and she can use her discovery to help a client. It's hard for her to explain how it happens. The numbers simply take shape, and the story forms.

Jen gets a call from one of her customers, and the customer isn't happy. It wasn't anything Jen did; it was a mistake the warehouse made. But Jen knows that she'll get this fixed. A sense of calm comes over her, and she knows just what to say and what to do to make everything OK again. She rallies her internal partners in the warehouse, and by the time the situation is resolved, her relationship with the customer is stronger than ever.

These are stories of strengths-based selling — different people using different innate and powerful abilities to get the same result: success.

Strengths Based Selling is about your strengths and your personal approach to sales. In this book, we will give you strategies and tips to help you use your strengths to increase your sales performance and to achieve success. We'll also share advice from some of the best salespeople we've ever met. *Strengths Based Selling* is meant to be comprehensive. We want it to be the essential how-to book for every kind of salesperson across all industries. But you must understand all the strategies, tips, and advice through your filter of the world — your talents and strengths.

Before we dive in, there's something you should know. We believe there are two widely held myths about sales and selling:

Myth #1: Anyone can sell. This myth keeps too many people in the wrong career. Only certain people have the ability to consistently perform well in sales. Those individuals have a rare combination of natural talent, skills, knowledge, and practice. Anyone with enough ambition can learn skills, acquire knowledge, and find opportunities to apply them. Without natural talent though, all the skills, knowledge, and practice in the world won't make a salesperson great.

In our work, it has become clear that talent is misunderstood and underappreciated. When most people talk about talent, they mean the ability to excel at things like hitting three-pointers from the top of the key, mastering the violin, or performing Shakespeare. Those definitions are too narrow. In reality, talent exists in each of us. And more importantly, it exists in each of us *differently*. For some of us, that talent applies to selling; for others, it simply doesn't.

Because the notion that anyone can sell is so widespread, organizations often hire people with little thought about the natural wiring they have — or don't have — for sales. After all, why bother with talent when anyone can be trained to sell? Why worry about talent when practice makes perfect? That's exactly why so many sales organizations have such a wide variation in performance from salesperson to salesperson, and nothing they do makes a long-term difference.

Myth #2: There's one right way to sell. That's nonsense. There is no plan, program, or technique that's guaranteed to boost sales — despite the guy you saw up on the stage at the last sales conference who said, "If you do it just like me, you'll succeed beyond your wildest dreams!" His approach works for him because it's based on his talents and his skills and knowledge, plus years of practice. In other words, if you *are* him, his way will work. But you're not. You can't copy his approach or anyone else's.

Does this mean you can't learn from other salespeople? Of course not. You can certainly gain insights from studying other people's success. The key, however, is to understand that you must take what you learn and make it work for you based on your own strengths. Sometimes you might find that what you learn doesn't work for you at all. "I've got buddies who are phenomenal golfers, and they've never taken a golf lesson in their life," said Dirk Tinley, a mortgage loan officer at U.S. Bank Home Mortgage. "I've spent thousands of dollars on golf lessons, and I'm just about as bad as the day I started."

It's important to recognize these sales myths for what they are. We wanted to challenge the conventional wisdom about sales because we know that these myths drag down performance. We've seen it over and over again in our own work with companies and in Gallup's research, and we've heard it straight from the best salespeople we've ever met (a few of whom you'll encounter in this book).

You've got your own talents and your own strengths, and you need to make them work for you. Yes, you need knowledge and skills, and you need practice. If you want to be a star salesperson, though, you need knowledge, skills, practice, and a *deep understanding of your talents*. You must maximize who you are rather than trying to make yourself someone else. Trying to be someone you're not is exhausting and dispiriting, and it leads to mediocrity.

In the following pages, you'll learn about talents and strengths. With help from the Clifton StrengthsFinder, you'll learn what your own talents are and get ideas about how to apply them to every step of the sales process, from cold calling to retaining customers. You'll learn the essentials of customer engagement and how to better engage your clients. And you'll learn what employee engagement is and how you can better engage yourself at work. Furthermore, you'll confront the problem of work/life balance and discover why the concept itself is sorely misguided.

Accepting the truth about sales — that not everyone can sell and that there are as many ways to sell as there are salespeople — is extremely liberating. If you enjoy sales, if you're good at it, and if you're finding some of the success you want, you possess a rare ability — and you should celebrate it. You're someone who can do this job. And if you're trying to follow a method or emulating a sales hero and it's not working, it might not be your fault. Who you are is who you should be. You'll be most successful at sales if you make the most of who you are.

A WORD TO SALES MANAGERS

Sales managers, this book is for you too. You are evaluated on the performance of your team, so the insights in this book should be as helpful to you as they are to your reps. *Strengths Based Selling* draws on decades of Gallup research documenting the performance improvements that result when employees use their talents and strengths. We have even more data regarding the symbiotic relationship of strengths and employee engagement, which itself propels performance. So, the more your people use their talents, the better they will sell, and the more engaged they will be.

But managers: You can't do it for them. You can only help your sales teams capitalize on the best of what they've already got. You'll find out how as you read on, but we encourage you to become familiar with your own talents and strengths before focusing on your salespeople's. Understanding and using your own talents will help you guide your people to use their talents to improve their performance. Take the time to better understand how your strengths contribute to your effectiveness as a manager. Just as we are helping salespeople achieve sales success through their strengths, you can achieve your own success — and your team's — through your talents and strengths.

Chapter 1:
Defining Strengths

THIS CHAPTER'S KEY POINTS

- Your talents are unique to you, and capitalizing on them improves performance.

- A strength is the ability to consistently produce a positive outcome through near-perfect performance in a specific task.

- Developing your natural talents into strengths takes hard work; when you add skills, knowledge, and practice, your natural talents become a multiplier in the strengths equation.

"When I took the Clifton StrengthsFinder and I got the results, I was floored by how dead on they were," said Baylor, a sales rep, of Gallup's talent assessment. "But here's the weird thing — I'd never given any thought to any of that stuff. I don't think I'd even noticed I had talents, and I sure didn't try making my talents *better*."

Baylor's realization is typical. Most of us lack perspective on our own talents. Do you really know who you are? Do you truly understand your talents and how to apply them to sales? We're betting that you don't, at least not as well as you could. Like most people, you probably need a better understanding of how to tap into your unique talents — and how they could give you an edge in your sales performance.

Gallup has studied performance in many professions for decades. In fact, one of the first groups Gallup ever studied was insurance salespeople in the late 1960s. Since then, we've interviewed and analyzed millions of people in hundreds of job roles in dozens of industries in countries all over the world. We paid close attention to those who were the best at their jobs. And we found that the best of the best are always different from the others. The same is true for great salespeople. Though they share many of the same traits, the best reps are very different from one another.

For instance, we recently met with the top 25 leaders of a big medical insurance sales team. When we asked them about the difference in performance between the company's top salespeople and all the rest, we found that the best salespeople were four times more productive than their colleagues. This company has hundreds of reps. Imagine what that difference means in dollars. Here's another example: We conducted an analysis of 250,000 sales reps working for 170 Gallup clients. The results showed that the top 25% of the sales force was responsible for generating an average 57% of year-over-year sales increases in their companies. On the other hand, the bottom 25% of the sales force was selling *less* than it had the year before.

We examined the data in every possible way to try to find an explanation for the startling variance in these sales results. The difference wasn't experience; we didn't study anyone with less than one year in the role. It wasn't education; the analysis showed that education didn't correlate to productivity. So why did some salespeople — who were like everyone else in many ways — perform so much better than others? The difference was *talent*. The best sales professionals had an unusual ability to build enduring and profitable relationships with clients, to close business, and to keep those relationships producing long term. That's a matter of talent.

THE STRENGTHS EQUATION

Your talents are innate. But talent alone doesn't make a strength. To develop your natural talents into strengths, you need to add skills, knowledge, and practice. These are all important and necessary parts of the strengths equation.

Talent (a natural way of thinking, feeling, or behaving)

Investment (time spent practicing, developing your skills, and building your knowledge base)

Strength (the ability to consistently provide near-perfect performance)

You will have the opportunity to take the Clifton StrengthsFinder to find out what your individual talents are. But before you do, let's define these terms:

A **talent** is a natural way of thinking, feeling, or behaving, such as the tendency to be outgoing in social situations. Talents exist naturally and cannot be readily acquired like skills and knowledge can. Gallup groups talents into 34 broad categories called themes, such as Achiever, Analytical, Competition, Relator, and Strategic. These themes manifest differently in everyone. Talent alone isn't sufficient for sales performance, however. Talent is a precondition to success, but it needs to be refined with skills, knowledge, and practice.

A **strength** is the ability to consistently produce a positive outcome through near-perfect performance in a specific task. Getting to this level of performance isn't easy, and talent is just the starting place; skills, knowledge, and practice are also crucial to boosting performance and achieving success.

A **skill** is the basic ability to move through the fundamental steps of a task. Skills can be acquired through formal or informal training. For example, knowing how to complete an expense report is a skill that is often taught in sales training.

Knowledge is information — it is what you know. Data about the market and details about products and services are examples of knowledge.

Practice is repetition — actively working on your talents. Just as you need practice to build a muscle when you're weightlifting, you need practice in addition to training and education, feedback from others, and experiences to help you build your talents into strengths.

When you work in an area of strength, you're at the top of your game. Your talent is always there, guiding your reactions to the world around you. By adding knowledge, skills, and practice, you refine your talents and make them more productive. But when you don't work in an area of strength, you won't get as far as you'd like.

"To me it's natural. I just do it," said TC Crafts, a center director at Jenny Craig. "[At my company] we work on our strengths and focus on everyone's talent, and [we] improve our skills and get knowledge from the training department." We hear words to that effect from many salespeople — talents seem natural. A furniture company rep told us, "I honestly think I was born to do this. I just can't imagine what I'd do with my life other than sales. And, not to brag, I'm the best account exec in my company. But I would be a total failure at this if I hadn't learned my product line, clients, and the industry inside and out."

TAKING THE CLIFTON STRENGTHSFINDER

To help you discover your talents, you can take a brief assessment called the Clifton StrengthsFinder. You will need the unique access code in the packet in the back of this book to take the assessment. During the assessment, you'll be asked to respond to a series of items. Answer them quickly because your top-of-mind reactions most accurately reflect who you are. After you complete the assessment, you'll receive a report listing your top five talent themes. Though everyone has some degree of talent in all 34 of the talent themes, the top five have the most impact on making you who you are.

It's crucial to remember that *all* talents are important, and they all can contribute to success in a sales career. Gallup has studied hundreds of thousands of salespeople, and we've seen all 34 talent themes in action. Top salespeople use their talents, no matter what they are, to the utmost. They're like professional athletes — some are great runners, some are great swimmers, and some are great hitters. They're all different in every way except one: They're better at what they do than everyone else.

Keep your StrengthsFinder report handy as you read this book. Once you understand your talents and learn how to combine them with skills, knowledge, and practice, you'll start to think about your job in a whole new way. You will gain perspective about your unique approach to sales. You'll get insights on managing your career and your life. You may even see where you've made some wrong turns. Most importantly, you'll start realizing how you can sell with your strengths. You'll see how using the talents you have — and understanding who you really are — will make you a better salesperson.

Chapter 2:
Strengths and Weaknesses

THIS CHAPTER'S KEY POINTS

- Strengths-based selling is the application of individual strengths to achieve sales success.

- A weakness is something that gets in the way of your performance or in the way of the performance of another person. You can't ignore your weaknesses, but you can use your strengths to manage them.

Now that you've taken the Clifton StrengthsFinder, you can start thinking about how you can combine your talents, skills, and knowledge and add practice to influence your capacity for success. The problem is that talents are often unrecognized or misunderstood, while skills, knowledge, and practice are overemphasized.

We live in a world that's obsessed with fixing weaknesses. In school, students are directed to spend the most time on their toughest subjects so they can become "well-rounded." Workplace performance reviews often focus on our "areas of opportunity," where we can presumably do better with more effort, training, or management attention. One paper products sales rep said it best: "All my boss ever wants to talk about is what I'm doing wrong. He never mentions what I'm doing right." Too many sales organizations, like too many institutions in general, neglect talents and focus on weaknesses. What's more, too many sales managers think that training will take care of everything.

TRAINING

Training is important. No one can walk into this profession and know what to do and how to do it without being taught. Sales can be complex. From the products, services, systems, and processes to the interpersonal dynamics, there is a lot to master. And you should be taught as much of that as possible.

But talent cannot be taught. You can't be trained into greatness at something that requires talent, such as negotiating. You can learn the skills to pace a negotiation meeting, and you can learn negotiation cues and psychology. But you can't learn to be fearless about asking clients to pay premium prices or confident enough to show that you'll walk away from a deal or assertive enough to push your prospect toward a decision. If you don't have much talent for negotiating, you might get a little better at it from learning negotiation skills, but if you *do* have talent for negotiating, you will get *much* better *much* faster.

We understand the frustration of managers who, when seeing uneven performance results, come up with scripts and playbooks and hand them to their reps. But trying to legislate behavior in an area where talent carries the day is not only futile, it can kill innovation. There's more than one way to do just about anything, and a script forces everyone to behave identically. That's the wrong type of training. Instead of following mandated steps, we recommend that aspiring salespeople learn the necessary skills and knowledge. Learn what you need to know to work in your company's system. Then practice the areas where you excel, because that will help you build strengths.

STRENGTHS

This brings us back to strengths. Remember, a strength is the ability to consistently produce a positive outcome through near-perfect performance in a specific task. Strengths-based selling is using your strengths to achieve sales success.

Take Marcy, for instance. Among her top five themes are Context (historical perspective) and Harmony (a preference for agreement). These might not seem like typical talent themes for a sales rep, nor does the fact that she graduated from college with a degree in philosophy. "The only job interview I could get was here," said Marcy, who works for a company that sells windows directly to home owners. On the first day of the training class, she was convinced that "this was the wrong place for me — it was super aggressive, and no one could speak a complete sentence without mentioning sports."

Her first day on the job, Marcy cried three times. By the fourth day, she could hold back the tears until she got home. On the fifth day, she gave up on her job and just went through the motions, knowing they were going to fire her soon anyway. "My last prospect of the day let me in, and the first thing I did was thank him profusely. *Not* a take-charge thing to do," said Marcy. "But I noticed he was growing orchids. I blurted out that we could make windows that don't let in any UV light, but we don't so that people can grow houseplants."

They got so caught up in chatting about orchids that Marcy forgot she was supposed to be pushing windows. And when she remembered, it seemed more like a helpful suggestion than a hard sell. "The thing is, orchids can't tolerate vast temperature differentials, but they do need a lot of light. And the homeowner was paying staggering gas bills. We complained about energy bills for a while, and then I started throwing out statistics regarding estimated energy savings."

Soon she was measuring windows and calculating replacement costs. Marcy wound up making the sale and went home dry-eyed. She did it by using her ability to take background information and link it to a viable solution for her customer. By the end of the year, she was in the top 15% of her team. As Marcy's story shows, your strengths maximize your abilities.

When you're working from strength, you find yourself in a state of flow, something research psychologist Mihály Csíkszentmihályi described as "being completely involved in an activity for its own sake. The ego falls away. Time flies. Every action, movement, and thought follows inevitably from the previous one, like playing jazz. Your whole being is involved, and you're using your skills to the utmost." When you're using an area of strength to its utmost, you feel energized, powerful, and even a little euphoric.

When you aren't working in an area of strength, things are more difficult. This often becomes evident in sales, or in any role, when a person does not have the talent for the job. Each step of the process feels like an ongoing struggle, and the results likely aren't there. When this happens — when you don't feel a natural flow, and the right partnerships don't facilitate success — your talents may not fit the role.

TURNING TALENTS INTO STRENGTHS

Now it's time to consider your talents and how to shape them into strengths. Think about the critical elements of your role — the things you'll get fired for if you don't do or don't do well. No doubt you have a sales target. You might have a quota of people you must meet with, and you may have a cold call quota too. You certainly have paperwork. What else? What are the activities you must do to keep your job? With that in mind, think about how your top five themes apply to the requirements of your sales role.

Let's use Pablo as an example. Pablo is a sales representative whose top five themes are Achiever, Analytical, Ideation, Focus, and Competition. When Pablo was asked to think through his top five themes and how they apply to his sales role, he said, "Achiever — I guess that's what makes me want to keep plugging away. Analytical — I suppose I use that to see how or if the customer needs what I'm selling. I use Ideation to find customers when I'm cold calling, which I hate, or to help people see how they could use our products. I have to do so much multitasking, but Focus keeps me on track; I know a lot of sales reps who get so scattered between customers, they never know what they're doing. Competition — that's easy. I want to win, and everybody in sales has to have that."

This is the lens through which Pablo sees his sales world. It will be different for each person; not every sales representative is motivated by competition, for example. Don't worry if you don't see perfect matches between your talents and your role right now. We just want you to start thinking about your talents and how you can use them to boost your performance. Here's a hint: Consider the parts of your job that you enjoy the most, the ones that put you in a state of flow. It's likely that in those moments, you are operating from your strengths.

You might also have talents that don't seem to match parts of your job. For instance, your talents may be oriented toward building deep relationships. But what if you're in a job that doesn't let you use those talents? If so, your job may be less satisfying for you — and it might be harder for you to stay engaged at work. There's nothing wrong with having mismatches like this, but you need to find a way to manage around these disparities and make yourself effective in spite of them. Consider how to maximize your talents and what you do best, then capitalize on that. And if there is no way you can be comfortable in your current role, consider moving to a different sales role that allows you to use your talents more effectively.

WEAKNESSES

The term "weakness" sounds bad. That's why so many books, training sessions, and development programs substitute words like "challenges," "areas of opportunity," "things you do less well," "trainabilities," or "derailers." But euphemisms like these aren't helpful to you or to your employer — and they aren't accurate.

A weakness is a lack or misapplication of knowledge, skill, or talent that negatively affects your performance or that of others. You can also think of weaknesses as barriers, because they get in the way of your performance. You might become resigned to working in an area of weakness, and you might find ways to minimize the negative impact. But you'll never enjoy it, and you'll probably never find yourself in a state of flow while working in an area of weakness.

Let's revisit Pablo. When Pablo reviewed his full theme report (which lists his 34 themes in rank order), he noticed that Empathy was his 30th theme. "I just stink at Empathy, which my wife could tell you," said Pablo. "And every time

I try to put myself in someone else's shoes, I get frustrated at *them*. That doesn't help the situation. I have learned to *pretend* to care about the things my clients care about. The truth is, I don't want to bother with thinking about them."

And why should he bother? Sometimes your job requires you to work in an area that isn't a strength for you — but it's only a weakness if it gets in your way or someone else's way. Pablo realized that for the most part, his lack of Empathy does not get in his way if he can figure out how to capitalize on his other talents. For example, concentrating his Analytical talents to gather data, assess the facts of a situation, and work logically toward a solution may help him appear caring to the customer.

That's why we asked you to think about your talents and your job role. The places where you saw a direct link between your talents and your role are your areas of opportunity — because they can become strengths if you develop them. The places where you don't see a direct link between your talents and your role could become areas of weakness if you don't manage them. If those areas are getting in the way of your job performance or disturbing your coworkers, then they matter, and you have to manage them.

To deepen your understanding of the talents you possess and the weaknesses that could get in your way, you can do a self-audit. Taking StrengthsFinder was the first step. The second step is to determine where you spend your time and energy — and what you get from your efforts. If it takes a disproportionate amount of time and effort to perform certain parts of your job and you still aren't doing them well, that's likely a weakness. And if your manager is demanding that you do everything perfectly, ask him or her what the most important outcome of your effort should be. You'll probably hear something like "generating revenue." Make sure that you're using your strengths and managing your weaknesses to achieve that goal.

Pablo, for example, is lousy at cold calls. He finds it difficult to imagine others' lives, even when he knows them well; empathizing with strangers is nearly impossible. To ease his manager's concern about his poor cold calling, Pablo took a direct approach. He showed his manager how spending too much time in his areas of weakness was costing the company. Pablo explained, "I told my manager, 'In the time I spent cold calling over the past six months, I could have been in 12 face-to-face meetings where I could analyze my customers' situations. My batting average for those meetings is one sale for every three meetings. Instead, I spent my time making 50 cold calls, only four of which resulted in meetings.' So I asked my manager if I could team up with someone better at cold calling than me. That way, we'd both win."

The key is to build a business case for focusing on your strengths and managing your weaknesses. We're guessing that telling your boss you can't do something because it doesn't feel like a strength won't work too well. Instead, prove that your strengths are valuable to your organization, and show your boss that you have a plan for managing areas where you struggle. Then your weaknesses won't seem so important.

That's just the beginning of the conversation. People who receive ongoing feedback about their strengths perform at higher levels. Gallup's research has found that when hospitality sales reps received coaching on their strengths, their volume per guest was 11% higher and their closing percentage was 6% higher on average than sales reps who didn't receive coaching on their strengths. In some sales roles, a percentage point up or down in performance translates into thousands of dollars — maybe more.

Now that you know what strengths are — and you've learned what your top five talent themes are — it's time to apply them to the sales process. We'll start at the very beginning: prospecting.

Chapter 3:
Prospecting

THIS CHAPTER'S KEY POINTS

- The steps to prospecting can be broken down to determine what you do well and what you need help with.

- Salespeople have to overcome call reluctance. The key is to recognize your reluctance for what it is, examine why you experience it, then think about the talents you can use to combat it.

- Making contact with a key prospect may require turning a "gatekeeper" into a promoter and advocate. Don't assume that someone isn't a valuable asset based on his or her position or title alone.

"On the first day of a training cycle, a sales manager always tells the newbies that sales is a numbers game," one rep told us. "The more prospects you talk to, the likelier you are to get meetings. The more meetings you take, the more proposals you make, the more proposals, the more sales. I've gotten way past my first training program, but the older I get, the more I have to admit that it's true."

We'd have to agree, though we'd also point out that the "numbers game" theory overlooks most of what creates sustainable high performance in sales. Nonetheless, prospecting — or looking for business where your company has no business yet — is an essential, if unpopular, part of the job for many sales reps. If prospecting, especially cold calling, isn't going well for you, it may be because your method isn't building on your strengths.

USING WHAT YOU HAVE

"I struggled with cold calling at first, but then I got good at it," said a hospitality sales executive. "And I got good by making some mistakes and by finding a comfort zone." People with certain themes in their top five may not feel reluctance to cold calling. They don't mind the battle of wills that is implicit in contacting a stranger and establishing a business relationship. They might even enjoy it. For example, if one of your leading talents is Command, cold calling might not be an issue for you. In fact, it might be a real thrill. Command compels you to confront challenge, to initiate, and to convince others to do something they probably weren't thinking they would do.

People with strong Woo talents look forward to extending themselves into the world to multiply their relationships. But Woo can also make rejection harder to accept. After all, Woo is about winning others over, and you won't be able to win over everyone you cold call. If you do have

Woo in your top five, however, you're likely to persevere because you'll be reluctant to give up until you've won someone over.

Those with Activator in their top five themes feel an impatience to get things moving and to get decisions made. These individuals will continue to cold call time and again. Those who lead with Competition have a desire to win, and you can't win if you don't dial the phone or walk in the customer's door. And Self-Assurance talents help people carry themselves with confidence — they assume they have the right to make the call or walk through the door.

People with themes in their top five that take a more contemplative approach — such as Ideation, Learner, Input, or Strategic — tend to use cerebral tactics, and starting out with a solution is a good way to catch a prospect's attention. "I have always looked for different ways of doing things," said a salesperson who has Strategic in his top five themes. "Whether it's a directive or a specific item to sell, I've always attempted to answer the question *why* first. Why did we create it? Why would the customer want it? I have to know *why* before I can convince anyone else."

Thinking through a calling list is just half the battle. You still need to engage the prospect and start the sales process. Some salespeople use their talents in themes such as Individualization, Empathy, Relator, or Communication to warm up the call. Others may use their Achiever, Activator, or Strategic talents to power through their initial conversations.

People with strong talents in some themes are more likely to be gregarious, friendly, and outgoing. Those who lead with Communication, Relator, Includer, Positivity, or Woo tend to enjoy talking to people and getting to know more about them. John Wells, senior vice president at Interface, is a good example. "I have Woo, Individualization, and Developer, so I wasn't intimidated with opening a door or making a cold call," he said. "I've loved it since I began."

But prospecting doesn't come that easy for some people. Sometimes the purpose of the call — the sale — feels like it gets in the way of building the relationship, at least to those who lead with their social skills. Though these salespeople may enjoy making friends out of strangers, the fact that their goal is to persuade may dampen their enthusiasm. Because that feeling is so unpleasant, these salespeople may want to rush through the sales call to the next step — the actual sale — or drag it out forever.

If this sounds familiar, use your talents to start building relationships through more targeted conversations. Your Responsibility, Activator, Focus, or Discipline talents can help you keep on target with your prospects. Analytical, Ideation, Arranger, or Context talents can help you find solutions and foster stronger goodwill with your customers or prospects.

Some themes, such as Achiever, Maximizer, Activator, or Competition, can become intense or magnified and may need to be managed as you're prospecting. "I try to control my Achiever because, well, I may spend time on things that aren't adding value," said Alain Tremblay, senior manager of business development at Standard Life. Often, reps with top themes such as Achiever find motivation in the "numbers game" of prospecting. They might not get the thrill of conquest that people with Command or Woo do, and they may not feel the fun of solving puzzles that people with Analytical or Arranger do. But because they are motivated to accomplish, they'll drive relentlessly through the prospecting list. What they gain is the satisfaction of getting things done. If you lead with your Achiever, Maximizer, Activator, or Competition talents, they will help you power through your list of names. But be careful: Don't focus on just getting through your list; focus on how getting your cold calls made will lead you toward a sale. Don't mistake activity (making calls) for productivity (making sales).

"We do a lot of cold calling, and it feels weird to me to call a stranger and start talking about one of the most important and personal aspects of his life, his investment plan," said one first-year financial services rep. "But we [took] StrengthsFinder, and then my manager sat down and showed me how to use my strengths. Significance — it doesn't matter if I've talked to those people before or not because my product *makes* me an important part of their lives. The Input theme — man, I can't learn enough about them, and cold calling is how I do it. And if none of that is motivating me that day, just *doing* it is doing something. I may not make any money, but I'm making checkmarks, and that's a start."

In short, all talent themes are helpful in different ways for different people. Every talent theme is valuable when you're prospecting because they can all be used to develop expansive relationships, a term we'll define in greater detail in Chapter 10. In addition to applying your natural talents to prospecting, you can measure your effectiveness and employ various techniques to increase your success.

MEASURE, MEASURE, MEASURE

One of the truisms of business is: You can't manage what you don't measure. A good way to measure how effective you are at prospecting is to keep track of your inbound and outbound calls, the number of people you talk to, and the outcomes of your conversations. Your ultimate goal is to land a sale, but your short-term outcome for prospecting is to get a meeting. We'll use phone calls as an example and illustrate how you can use a tracking sheet to gauge your success rate.

Keep it simple, and track only initial contacts or cold calls. When you are prospecting, keep track of each time you pick up the phone and dial. (See "Sample Tracking Sheet")

Whether you get voice mail or a real human being, every phone call you make earns you a mark in the "Outbound Calls" column of your tracking sheet. In the "Contacts" column, note the calls that resulted in a conversation with someone. For the purposes of this exercise, don't judge the quality of that conversation. All that matters is that it was a live conversation.

At the end of two or three weeks, calculate your *contact rate*: the number of contacts you made divided by the total number of calls you made during the same time frame. That percentage will show you the success rate of your cold calls. This will help you see if you're making a large number of calls that don't result in conversations. If that's the case, maybe you should try calling at different times of the day, or maybe your list is bad, or perhaps you need to work on the messages you leave.

Building toward greater sales success involves increasing your numbers — boosting the number of calls you make, increasing your success at making contact, and improving your contact rate. To further enhance your effectiveness, keep track of the number of conversations that result from your contacts, and compare that to your contact rate. You can calculate your *conversation rate* by dividing the number of conversations by the number of contacts you made. Comparing your conversation rate to your contact rate helps you see how effective you are at cold calling.

SAMPLE TRACKING SHEET

	Outbound Calls (number of times you picked up the phone and dialed)	Contacts (people you talked to)	Conversations (discussing your product or service with someone)
Monday	15	4	1
Wednesday	12	3	2
Friday	19	8	4
Monday	9	7	3
Wednesday	16	5	2
Friday	15	3	1
Monday	18	8	3
Wednesday	13	6	2
Friday	6	3	1
Total	123	47	19

Contact rate: 47 contacts divided by 123 calls = 38%

Conversation rate: 19 conversations divided by 47 contacts = 40%

How are your scores? Are they improving, remaining static, or declining? Many sales professionals find that the simple act of keeping score helps them manage tasks that they otherwise might dread. To improve your contact or conversation rates, consider some of the techniques we discuss below.

Determining whom to call. The first step to increasing your odds of success is to figure out the right person or people to call. "First, do your research. I can't stress that enough," said one rep. "You need to know who the decision maker is, because the person making the decisions in that organization can eventually swing business your way — or somebody else's way, for that matter." You'll save time and increase your sales if you target the right people from the start.

Call reluctance. Whatever your talent themes, most salespeople must overcome call reluctance in one way or another. That's understandable. When you pick up the phone, you don't know what reception you'll get. Before you open that door for the first time, you don't know what you're walking into. You might get rejected, which eventually affects even reps with the thickest skin.

First, recognize call reluctance for what it is, then examine why you experience it. Think about the talents, skills, and knowledge you bring to combat it, and practice ways to work through it. In the end, you must get past call reluctance and make that call or open that door. A smart way to do that is to gather an arsenal of skills, such as getting past gatekeepers and warming up a cold call. You also need to do your homework so you have a well-thought-out and appropriate value proposition.

Value proposition. Rookie salespeople often have call reluctance because they don't know how to react if a live human prospect answers the phone. Surprisingly, this is also not unusual even among seasoned reps. All salespeople — new and experienced — can overcome call reluctance by creating and rehearsing the delivery of a value proposition. "You need some hook at the beginning that's actually legitimate as opposed to manipulative," said Geoff Nyheim, a successful sales veteran and vice president at Microsoft Online Services. "You're not just picking up the phone, which is what so many think cold calling is. You're preparing. You're getting that message together."

Regardless of your selling style, prospecting is supposed to create interest and to differentiate your offerings. A value proposition does that. To craft an effective one, answer these questions:

- How will your product/service help the prospect solve a problem, increase quality, or boost revenues?

- How will it help the prospect's company operate more effectively or reduce expenses?

- How will it help the prospect make a greater impact with his or her customers?

Simply put, before making contact, answer the question "What's in it for me?" from the prospect's point of view. Then you'll be ready to provide evidence that your company's product or service can do what your prospect needs it to do. Developing and rehearsing your pitch will increase your confidence and effectiveness and put teeth in your approach. Be sure to write the value proposition, edit it, then edit it again so that it has punch and sounds natural. Then practice, practice, practice.

Getting past "gatekeepers." One great cold caller we know had perhaps the best advice for getting past gatekeepers: Don't think of them as gatekeepers. Those administrative assistants who get between you and the prospect don't have to be obstacles. They can become promoters and advocates. Use your talents to enlist their help in making the sale.

One sales rep we spoke to was once an administrative assistant, which gives her a unique perspective. "Sometimes sales reps would suck up to me, and sometimes they'd ignore me," she said. "But the ones who got through me were the ones who convinced me that they could be important to my boss. I remember that every time I make a cold call."

Now that she's a sales rep herself, she takes the time to get to know the gatekeeper, and she never calls without a good reason. "I use what I learn from my research when I talk to gatekeepers," she said. "For instance, I work with car dealership chains. When the government started the cash-for-clunkers [program], I got on the phone quick and told all the admins that I needed to talk to their bosses before the rebate ended." That gave the gatekeepers their own sense of urgency, which they translated to their bosses.

Remember, part of the gatekeepers' job is to help their bosses make the best use of their time. Your job is to convince those gatekeepers that one of the best things their bosses can do is spend time talking to you. Gatekeepers can become your advocates if you treat them just like you would treat a prospect. So you need a pitch — shorter and punchier — to deliver just to them.

"In this industry, generally you're not meeting the C Suite first," said Rita Robison, senior vice president at Jones Lang LaSalle, an international commercial real estate company. "You meet people who, while they're tied in, aren't really the decision makers. The sooner you learn that in your career, the better. The person who got sent out to meet you, though, can be somebody whose respect you really need, because he or she is the person who goes back and tells the corporate treasurer or the CEO about you."

Setting prices. In most cases, the prospecting call is not the right time to start talking price — you want to be selling value. Your prospect might want to get a look at the sticker price before continuing a conversation with you, however. Be careful what you say. Many salespeople lowball during this part of the conversation, thinking they can upsell the prospect later. Often, the opposite is true. They unwittingly set the price, and it's not the one they meant to use.

What they're doing is called "anchoring." In 2002, Princeton psychology professor Daniel Kahneman was awarded the Nobel Prize in Economics (though he's not an economist — he's a psychologist) for integrating insights from psychology into economics. His research centers on the way people make decisions. Kahneman tested various situations and discovered that humans tend to look for and subconsciously accept a set price — an anchor — which is usually the first price named. In the case of sales, customers use that anchor as a midpoint to scale negotiations down or up. No matter where the conversation goes, that anchor is always in the back of a prospect's mind.

So always name the highest price you reasonably can when price discussions begin, because that price becomes an anchor. Then you come down on the price, if necessary, when negotiating. When you start with your highest price and negotiate down, regardless of what the final price is, the customer will remember the anchor price and feel that he or she has saved money.

Warming up the cold call. Sometimes prospecting means cold calling, and all cold calls start with an introduction. You state your name, your organization, what you're selling, and why. Once you've gotten that out of the way, the cold call isn't so cold anymore. But you don't have to make the introduction in person. You can start inserting yourself in your customer's world with a letter or an e-mail. A good introductory letter, for example, should be customized, based on the research you've done on the company, make a compelling business case, and present a valid value proposition.

The introductory letter should go something like this:

Dear [NAME],

My company and XYZ were in discussions years ago about potential partnerships. Since then, we have continued to grow and conduct an increasing amount of business in your industry.

As the new sales executive in the region, I revisited some of our past opportunities in your industry and ran across your comments in an annual report — your first at XYZ at the time. I was impressed with your commitment to operating efficiency and making XYZ world-class. Many companies pay lip service to the idea of efficiency, but you seem to really mean it.

My company has helped many of your peers achieve improved financial performance. In fact, our business impact in this area is unparalleled.

I know there are ways we can add value to and accelerate your efforts to differentiate XYZ and win big in your industry. Our partnership could support you to achieve your goal of 10% annual growth in earnings per share.

I am sending your vice president this information as well. Please let me know what you think — and when I can discuss this with you in more detail.

Warm regards,

Then there's the approach used by Steve Sieck, a sales director from Pfizer. His top five themes include Woo and Communication, which ought to work wonders in a cold call, but they failed him with a prospect when he tried using them over the phone. So he used those themes in a persuasive letter instead. "This doctor worked at an office where they were great at turning reps away, and it just killed me," Steve said. "So I finally sent him a letter with a picture of me and my family. I wrote, 'This is my family. I'm very proud to work for Pfizer. I'm proud to represent these products. It's my job to talk to you, so my hope is that you'll call me and see me.' And what do you think he did? He [met with] me."

Once you've sent the letter, your job has just begun. You can't assume that your prospects received the letter — or read the letter if they received it. You need to be prepared for responses to both situations when you make your follow-up contact by phone or in person. If your prospect hasn't read the letter, be ready to summarize it using a crisp value proposition. If the prospect has read the letter, gauge his or her interest and move toward the next steps — providing further information, offering to set up a meeting, or other appropriate follow-up.

Warming up a cold call with a letter can increase your chances of success. When you follow up personally, you show the prospect that you're checking back in. This way, the prospect has had a chance to ponder your product or service. That will save you time and energy — and increase your odds of getting a meeting.

STRENGTHS APPLIED: PROSPECTING

Here are some ideas for prospecting using specific talent themes. Now think about your talents and strengths, and come up with some ideas for how you can improve cold calling and prospecting using your own top five themes.

1. Example: Belief

    You must believe in what you're selling. Look for reasons why what you sell matters. How is it going to make the lives of your customers better? Also consider how successful cold calls are making life better for the people who matter most to you.

2. Example: Analytical

    Take the time to boil down the most compelling aspects of what you sell. Know your product or service better than anyone else. Your own insights about what you sell will help you see how you can benefit the people you cold call. As you gain experience about the relevance of your product, be sure to apply it to the prospect's situation.

3. Example: Arranger

    Organize your approach to calling to keep you energized. While cold calling, perform other activities that won't distract you but that will keep your mind active: organize files or jot down notes. Your Arranger often wants to do more than one thing at a time.

4. Example: Significance

    Tie your cold calling to great achievement. Focus on how successful cold calling will ultimately set you apart from those who cannot master it. Set lofty objectives about connecting with people whom others can't reach. And when you succeed, let someone close to you know about your achievement.

5. Example: Includer

    Frame cold calling as a way to bring someone into an opportunity from which they were previously excluded. Realize that without connecting to you, these individuals would not be exposed to the information and the relationships that you're bringing to the table. Also think about "who knows who" in the prospect's organization.

Chapter 4:
Assessing Opportunity

THIS CHAPTER'S KEY POINTS

- By effectively applying your talents and strengths when assessing opportunity, you can learn how to determine — and increase — your odds of success.

- Building lasting connections with people who can influence the prospects you're trying to connect with will improve your odds.

- Some basic guidelines are: talk to the right person, forecast your chance of success, recognize buying signals, understand soft closes, assess the competition, learn the customer's decision-making process, calculate the customer's switching cost, and learn the customer's culture.

- Part of being successful is recognizing bad business and knowing when to walk away.

In conducting scores of focus groups with great salespeople over the past four decades, Gallup researchers have heard many illuminating observations about sales. We heard such a gem while conducting research with a group of top account executives at one of the world's leading software companies. The company hires sales professionals with apparent promise, yet some of them don't pan out. Why? We asked the seven account executives why good people fail at that company. "It's because those reps chase bad opportunities," one sales rep said as the others nodded. "You have only so much time. You have to know when a pursuit just isn't worth it. Some people don't know when it's time to quit."

The researchers probed further, asking the executives how they know when it's time to walk away. The group members described an innate ability to look dispassionately at opportunities and to compute the odds for success. They said that many unsuccessful salespeople not only fail to do that, but they also chase the wrong chances, incur substantial opportunity costs, and waste time and resources that could be better directed at other pursuits.

They were right about every point. In many sales arenas, focusing on matching your product to your prospect instead of assessing your overall sales opportunities wastes valuable time. "I pulled the plug on a prospect recently. It was a huge risk, but I just didn't feel like he was emotionally invested to the extent that would be required for [the deal]," one rep told us. "This was a huge decision of mine that people might have gotten fired for. But I just didn't feel he was emotionally invested."

EVALUATING OPPORTUNITY

Salespeople must be able to evaluate prospects and decide which ones to pursue. That sounds like a basic research project, and it is. But don't assume that there is only one way to do prospect analysis. All talents and strengths can be useful, and you will do better at gauging opportunities if you apply your unique talents to the job. While some salespeople may be calculating the prospect's financials and stock market evaluations, others might take a completely different approach.

For example, if your top five themes include Self-Assurance, Command, or Activator, you can push people to take action. If you lead with these talents in your sales activities, you're likely the kind of person who gets things done, and that's great. But the need to get started or to take action might blind you to the pitfalls of a prospect. So don't let these talents shortchange the evaluation process. Instead, use them *in* the process to find real opportunities and to keep yourself and your team motivated.

If you have strong Relator, you may look for ways to foster and sustain relationships over time. You might ask prospects about their team, their customers, and even their family. You might also notice how much an executive assistant shares about her personal life or whether or not members of a team eat lunch together consistently. These important emotional insights allow you to use your Relator talents to cultivate relationships that matter.

Emotions play a key role in how people make decisions. Salespeople who have a talent for sensing the underlying emotional aspects of a potential sale can be adept at assessing prospects and knowing how to move them toward a decision. If you lead with Empathy or Individualization, you might be very good at perceiving a prospect's emotional needs — essentially, sensing the buying style of the customer. Knowing that buying style might give you an edge. You can pick up clues that others miss.

"You need to know what you're setting out to do, what the steps are, and who's going to do them," said Rita Robison from Jones Lang LaSalle, whose top five themes include Input and Learner. "I'm constantly using the resources around me, and that's something that I have to teach a lot of the youngest reps — get up, walk down there, and ask, 'What's the cost of drywall per linear foot today?' Let's ask property management, let's ask the guys in sales. Let's ask corporate finance, let's find out." That's exactly what you'd expect to hear from someone with Learner and Input, and Rita is using both to research her opportunities. She demonstrates how curiosity leads to asking the right questions.

Gauging opportunities through information gathering can help you see situations for what they are. "When I meet people for the first time, I try to interact with them. I try to let them do more talking; I do information gathering," said Ron Barczak, a sales rep from Stryker. "I am not one to go in and try to wow you with my blazing personality. I want to figure out what are you doing. I'll take that information and formulate it into a game plan and try to give you some solutions that can help you. Maybe I can help you save some money or do something more efficiently or easier. It's about developing a game plan of how we're going to try to work together — or if we even *want* to work together." If slowing down to investigate and gain perspective isn't your strong point, it might be a good idea to develop a complementary partnership with someone who excels at it. Use these partners as a sounding board to help you calculate your odds of success. (You can learn more about complementary partnerships in the Appendix.)

BUILDING RELATIONSHIPS

Knowing how to apply your talents to assessing opportunity is a tactical advantage. But evaluating opportunity also requires knowledge and solid skills. As a sales rep, it's critical for you to learn how to determine the difference between a real opportunity to sell and a place that will just give you a meeting.

In some sales organizations, the number of meetings a salesperson gets is an important part of the performance review. There might be a quota for "number of client meetings scheduled" or "customers met." Ratings like these are related to the numbers game. And yes, the more meetings you get, the more likely it is that you'll get to the decision maker, the more decision makers you will meet, and the more sales you will make.

But you must also consider the odds of creating a relationship with a prospect. How likely is it that you'll eventually form a solid relationship? Will you be sitting in meetings until the end of time? Or does the customer's behavior and history suggest that your efforts will result in a productive relationship?

"When you're devoting a year — or two or three — to business development or the relationship, you'd better really understand who's strong, who is going to be there," said Mike Astrauskas, a sales representative from Cargill. Strategic is one of his top five themes, and he uses it to assess the time and effort that building a client relationship will take. "Don't get me wrong. It's not like business is that easy to come by, but I look at it as an investment in time and a relationship. If you're going to keep spending time and effort, it had better be with people you can really be engaged with."

You've assessed whether you've got a good opportunity. You've figured the odds of developing a solid relationship. You've set up the first meeting. Now what? Now you need to know some basic facts, and even experienced account executives can use a refresher: talk to the right person, forecast your chance of success, recognize buying signals, understand soft closes, assess the competition, learn the customer's decision-making process, calculate the customer's switching cost, and learn the customer's culture.

INCREASING YOUR ODDS FOR SUCCESS

You've got a good opportunity for a sale, and you're confident you can develop a solid relationship. Here are some basic tips to build that relationship at the first meeting and beyond.

- Talk to the right person.

- Forecast your chance of success.

- Recognize buying signals.

- Understand soft closes.

- Assess how you stack up to your competitors.

- Learn the customer's decision-making process.

- Calculate the customer's switching cost.

- Learn the customer's culture.

Talk to the right person. The days of a single economic decision maker are over in most companies and industries. Even some small businesses make decisions in groups. Are you talking to the right person or people? Whom do most of your client influencers and advocates report to? Who has sign-off authority for the price you're going to quote?

Forecast your chance of success. Realistically assess your likelihood to hit pay dirt with your prospects. Are they expressing a need for your products or services? Is that need strong enough that they're willing to pay your price? Is there a competitor entrenched in the prospect's organization? You should consider many factors. If you lead with Analytical or Strategic, this may happen instinctively. If you don't, talk about your opportunities with your manager and colleagues, and have them weigh in on your odds of success. If there's a 10% chance, that prospect is worth only 10% of the time you're allotting to companies at this stage of the sales process. If the odds are 90%, go all in, as you'll be able to close and move on to other prospects soon.

Recognize buying signals. "I had a colleague, a young sales guy who was so knowledgeable, he was just incredible, and he went all the way through this whole sales blitz," said an energy industry account executive. "Finally, he came to a pause, and I looked at the purchasing agent, and the PA was ready. You could tell! And I'll be darned but our sales guy took off and started selling again. He went off on something else we could do. So the second time he stopped, I looked at the PA again and could tell he was getting impatient. The sales guy was still thumbing through things, and I knew he was going to start in again, so I jumped in and said, 'So do we need a purchase order for your business?' And the PA said, 'Yes, you do. Let me get it for you.' On our way out, I told the sales guy, 'It's nice to be knowledgeable about what you're doing, but eventually you have to let them buy.'"

Understand soft closes. Soft closes are the most comfortable for everyone. That's because in a soft close, the sale is never asked for — it's inevitable. "I have what I call an implied close. I don't ever ask for the order," said Ron Barczak from Stryker. "During [the sales] process, if I've done my job right and I've disclosed the information, the options, and the timeline that you need to purchase something, I've [pitched] my close throughout the whole interaction. So there doesn't have to be a magic moment where I've got to ask for the order. You get it to a certain point where it just kind of flows."

Use a soft close when you have an ongoing relationship with the customer or when your customer isn't considering or currently using one of your competitors. Use a hard close when there's a deadline looming, such as a budget closing, or when you have a competitor you're trying to keep out or replace. But consider the situation carefully before going for a hard close: When a possible piece of business might provide an opportunity for a creative partnership with the client, pushing hard for a close might actually land you a smaller deal than you would have gotten moving at a slower, softer pace.

Assess how you stack up to your competitors. This part of the process requires basic research so you have a working knowledge of your competitors. Read their websites. Your competitors probably haven't read theirs recently — and have you checked *your* organization's website lately? Talk to people who have worked for them. Talk to your customers who have done business with them. Ask your customers, "Are you working with someone else on this? How's that going for you?" This gives you a more robust view of your offering in relation to the competition.

The goal is for you to gain a deep understanding of the competition that gets you beyond their marketing jargon to a direct relationship with the customer. This is important: Superficially, your competitors may seem to offer the same thing you do. But if you look closer — and talk to the competition's clients about their experience with those competitors — you'll find areas where you can differentiate your message. Exploit them. That way, as you're crafting a value proposition, you can make it unique to the customer — and better than your competitors'.

Learn the customer's decision-making process. When selling big-ticket items, you'll invest a significant amount of your company's time and resources in a deal. Knowing how decisions are made can save you a lot of trouble. That's why understanding the customer's decision-making process shouldn't be left to the end; you should be learning it as you're qualifying the opportunity. Sometimes purchasing decisions are structured and formal, while other times they're ad hoc. The process has little to do with the size of the customer's organization. Often, it depends on how centralized the organization is. But it has a lot to do with how you'll get the sale.

Early on, ask prospects how they make decisions and how many people are involved with budgeting, implementation, and related issues. Recognize that decisions are rarely made by an individual. And remember: Most organizations and individuals are risk averse, so expect that a group of people will have to reach a consensus about purchases. You can help them generate that consensus by getting the right people at the client organization talking about what you sell. Just asking about their decision-making process may start them down the path of buying. You may find it useful to document the process and send it back to them, which confirms the road you're on. You might even design the document to look like a contract, stipulating the process and making it clear that it will culminate in a sale.

If the customer bristles when you ask about the decision-making process, it might mean she's not in buying mode, or you might be talking to someone who doesn't actually have the power to buy. That doesn't mean the sale is doomed, but it does call into question whether the customer is serious and whether you are talking to the right people in the organization.

Calculate the customer's switching cost. It's good to know what the switching cost is, but it can be difficult to determine because there may be variables that you can't know about. In some industries, switching costs are significant and can include everything from transitioning to a new system, implementation, training, and down time to remodeling the organizations' buildings. If you can't ascertain the exact switching cost, it's important to talk with the customer about it. You'll gain insight into the company, you'll show you care, and you may find opportunities to present solutions they haven't considered.

Learn the customer's culture. Knowing how the organization operates gives you an enormous advantage: You'll know how to present yourself and your product, you'll know whom to talk to and how, you'll know where the barriers are and how to get around them, and you'll have a much better feel for the office politics.

One salesperson said that he never goes to meetings alone. He needs at least one other person to scout. While he's busy selling, his scout watches the customers' body language and observes the cultural cues of the office. Afterward, they synthesize what they've learned about the client's culture.

So start paying attention at the very first meeting. Does the client wear Brooks Brothers ties? That says something about how he wants to be perceived. Does she make you wait, or does she come out to greet you? Is his office full of books, trophies, and family photos? Does everybody leave for lunch, or do they eat at their desks? Is the company hierarchical? Does the company seem to have a generous budget, or is frugality the norm? Are employees punctual? Just as in poker, details like this are "tells," and smart salespeople look for them and use what they learn.

WHEN TO WALK AWAY

If you apply your talents and a little sophistication in assessing opportunity, you'll increase your odds of success. You'll spend more time making sales and less time wondering why you're not. And you may find yourself giving up a little more often — and that can be a good thing. "In sales, you need to be clear, you need to know how to read people, you need to develop trust, and you need to know when to stop and move on," said Steve Sieck from Pfizer.

That may seem counterintuitive, but it's crucial. Salespeople are taught to be persistent, to overcome objections, to stick with it, and to win. Many sales reps share this approach, and they need to. Sales requires determination and the ability to shrug off rejection. But there is such a thing as smart time management, and wise salespeople recognize futility.

"A face-to-face call is extremely costly. [It's] not just the actual cost of your time and getting you there, but [it's] the opportunity cost — to call on somebody and not on somebody else," said one rep. "So it's paramount for account executives to be effective at assessing an opportunity. You'll survive or not as a salesperson just by how well you do this. Having a solid, specific selling process that filters out the wrong customers is extremely important to be successful."

STRENGTHS APPLIED: ASSESSING OPPORTUNITY

Here are some ideas for assessing opportunity using specific talent themes. Now think about your talents and strengths, and come up with some ideas for how you can assess opportunities more effectively using your own top five themes.

1. Example: Ideation

   Think beyond the obvious. When working to understand different ways to get in the door, look for a more obscure route that your competition has missed. What is a unique angle for your product or service? Who are you missing as a door opener? Who is connected throughout the organization but in a less noticeable manner? Get creative. Brainstorm lots of potential avenues.

2. Example: Deliberative

   Take time to assess what you think the customer really needs that you can provide. Anticipate roadblocks, and have rebuttals in mind. Investigate what you know about the competition, products currently in the marketplace, and the prospect's ability to buy. Slowing down the sales cadence can help you consider whether or not you should pursue the sale.

3. Example: Self-Assurance

Help clients and colleagues lean on the confidence you bring to a situation. As you assess opportunity, look for ways to make recommendations that the competition is uncomfortable making. Your job as a salesperson is to help. Show the customer that you know you can help differently than others can.

4. Example: Command

Take the lead for the customer whenever possible. When you see a chance to handle something that will enrich your understanding and build on an opportunity, take it. By stepping up, you will gain more access, and this will give you the inside track for seeing opportunities. Make recommendations when appropriate.

5. Example: Learner

Build a deep reservoir of knowledge about your clients — not just their products and services, but their people too. Who can help you build on this opportunity? Who is connected deeply throughout the organization? Who has access to the information you need to make a difference? Find the answers to these questions, and you will position yourself solidly.

Chapter 5:
Identifying Solutions

THIS CHAPTER'S KEY POINTS

- You don't need to know all the answers, but you do need to ask the right questions. Often, asking great questions will generate dialogue. Your findings will allow you to provide solutions — not just products, but information, advice, and insights — that your customers need, even if they don't realize they need it.

- Putting the customer first means that sometimes you won't be the right person for the job. Getting your customer to the right person or resource can be a critical step in building a stronger partnership.

- To ensure that your solutions offer real value, you need to understand your customers' business and priorities. By providing customized solutions, you position yourself as a valued partner, not just a vendor.

- Preparation is key. Understanding the price and scope of solutions *before* you discuss them with your customers will build credibility and increase your chances of success.

We spoke to a retired account executive, Ray, who had spent his career selling concrete equipment. When he talked about the sales rep who had trained him, we could tell that Ray was still in awe of him decades later. "This guy was amazing. He had an uncanny ability to figure out what people needed," Ray told us. "He would go out to the site and just look around, asking the guys all kinds of questions about how their day was going, if the new [product] was working out, if so-and-so's wife had had the baby. Then he'd find the boss and ask more questions. By the time he was done, he had a list ready of what the crew needed now, what they'd need in a couple of weeks, and what they would need if bids A, B, and C came through."

Long after Ray was selling on his own, he would go out on calls with his former trainer just to watch him work. "It was always an education," Ray said. "I still don't know how he did it, but I know this: He taught me the difference between selling and taking orders."

We don't know what Ray's trainer's talent themes were, but what matters is that he was using his talents to find solutions for problems that customers didn't know they had. And he wasn't making simple logical matches between his products and what the customers thought they needed. In a logical match, the salesperson assumes that the customer needs what he's got to sell, and that's that. It doesn't require much research, insight, or knowledge to make a logical match. It's a simple pairing: their need, his product.

Solutions, however, are different. To find a solution, you don't need to know all the answers, but you do need to ask the right questions. Geoff Nyheim from Microsoft Online Services had some good questions that salespeople should ask: What are the CEO's business priorities? What press releases has the business issued, and what interviews have the senior executives been doing? How do those activities reflect the business' priorities? How does all this information translate into an offering you can give customers to achieve one of their stated priorities or to solve a pressing problem? What value levers are at play? What things can you measure, such as revenue, customer engagement, and inventory turns? Can you arrive at a mutual definition of the opportunity? And do you think about the solution in a similar way?

"It's very important to make sure you have the same value levers," said Geoff, who has Strategic, Input, and Maximizer in his top five themes. "Cost avoidance and top-line revenue generation are two different things." The goal is to find a solution that works for your clients — even if finding that solution means sending them to a competitor. It hurts when that happens, but when customers see this selfless behavior, they realize that you really do have their best interests in mind.

"I can't tell you the number of times that I get calls from customers who say, 'Ron, I know you don't sell this, and I'm sorry to bother you, but I know you'll know where I should go for it,'" said Ron Barczak from Stryker. "And I say, 'Listen, you call me every single time, because if I don't know how to answer it, I will know who can. I have no problem with you calling me for everything, even when I don't benefit.'" Ron conceded, "That's a double-edged sword, but I would rather have them calling me than calling my competitors and asking them the same question."

KNOWLEDGE IS POWER

The first step to finding solutions is differentiating your customers and knowing them individually. Picture the "operating space" between you and the customer. The operating space is a way of thinking about your relationship or connection with that client. This space needs to be full of quality "stuff." One mistake that reps make is thinking they should fill that space by throwing their own answers into it. This results in every customer's space looking exactly the same no matter who the customer is.

Instead, the operating space should clearly belong to each customer and should be built on a foundation of information and insights that come from the customer. You begin to fill that space by asking the right questions and listening closely to the answers. Then, you layer on ideas, discoveries, and solutions that bond you to the customer. At first, you may think that the only value you bring to that space is through your answers. Instead, recognize that good questions can give your customers new ways to view their world — which in turn can give you new opportunities to deepen your relationships and increase sales.

"The real magic lies in how you stay in touch and what else you can do to [get] that relationship closer to producing revenue for you," said a hospitality industry rep. "Once you get that in your blood and you realize that you're pretty good at this, you see that every opportunity is 'hero time' for salespeople." This rep's Significance theme is at work here. It compels him to have a big impact on the client. And he's smart to realize that he should develop a close relationship with his customer. That way, he knows what "stuff" to put in the operating space.

To stay one step ahead of the customer's needs, you need to think and behave proactively. And for that, you need information. Rita Robison from Jones Lang LaSalle believes that when salespeople lose business, about half the time it's because they didn't keep asking questions of a customer or prospect. "I [lead with] Learner. I'm always willing to admit that I don't know everything, and I don't have a fear of asking. I don't feel like I'm going to look stupid," she said. "So I don't mind asking questions. I'd rather know more than guess."

The right people to question aren't always decision makers, though. One mistake that many sales reps make is dismissing the importance of people who could influence the decision maker. This could be an individual who has the ear of a key decision maker or an administrative person who is at the center of an important communication chain. Salespeople need to listen carefully to all of their contacts in the company.

The solutions you suggest can be more than products; you can offer advice and insights too. You can provide perspective and knowledge the customer doesn't have but needs. Sometimes this is information they know they need and request from you. But other times, it can be information they don't know they need — facts or insights you offer in response to what you've heard in your conversations with your customers and company contacts.

Sometimes reps have access to information that's also readily available to customers, but they haven't discovered it yet. When was the last time you did a Web search on your most important customer or looked at that customer's website? A quick review of information that's available online could give you insights into the organization's most urgent problems or concerns. An e-mail with a nugget of helpful information shows clients that you're thinking about them, even when it doesn't result in an immediate sale.

As for gaining insights, start *before* you meet with your customers. You can't have useful insights if you don't know much about their business. Look at the customer's industry, competition, and demographics. Pull together everything you can get your hands on, and put yourself in your customer's shoes. "Every day is a school day, and I always want to learn and become an expert in whatever I'm doing," said Ron Barczak from Stryker. "When I was a college intern at a neon sign company, I asked the engineer to show me how the product worked, how it was built, how they made it, all that. I want to be the expert for the customer."

Mike Astrauskas from Cargill, sounding exactly like someone making the most of his Strategic theme, said, "It's been tough lately, so [our customers are running] lean and mean, and they don't have a lot of time and people to devote to understanding a solution. So when you go in there, you'd better understand their business, know the context as it applies to your product, and know where the value is for them. Each time we meet with a customer, we apply our innovation and technology to their business specifically. It's not saying, 'Here's what it is,' but, 'Here's the value of this to you.' We put into context not just money but the psychological benefits: 'Hey, you're doing the right thing. You guys want to be the most innovative. This is going to help you be the most innovative and keep you out in front of your competition.' They understand it, and they feel good about doing business with us. And now I think they truly value us as strategic [partners] to their business."

Mike nailed it. The best solutions are strategic, and the sales rep who can be part of the strategy becomes a valued partner, not just a vendor. We'll talk more about the difference between being a partner and a vendor later in this book. Your talents can help you build this new level of value with your customers. For example, are you an asker or a teller? If you lead with Command or Self-Assurance, you might find that you tell more than you ask. If that's the case, use one of your people-oriented themes to connect with someone who invites you to ask questions. Lean on your Futuristic theme to ask your clients where they want to be in 10 years. Customers need more than products.

They need solutions, strategies, emotional connections, and insider information. Providing that mix will take all your talents. "Don't go in unarmed," said Rita Robison from Jones Lang LaSalle. "The client's looking to you as the expert."

BUILDING INTERNAL PARTNERSHIPS

Sometimes finding the right solution for your customer is easy — marketing or R&D has just the thing for your client. But sometimes, you must dig deep in your own company to provide what your customer needs. Think about the operating space between you and your fellow employees. Again, this is a way for you to visualize the relationship and the things that go into that relationship. To get what you need for your customer, your coworkers must understand your customer as well as you do, and they should want to provide solutions as strongly as you do. This requires you to develop the same level of close partnerships we've been talking about, but internally.

Increasing the breadth and depth of your partnerships inside your organization is crucial to providing client solutions. Make your fellow employees see themselves as an integral part of that process. Ask them great questions instead of barking orders at them. Invite and involve rather than demand. To build your partnerships, treat your fellow employees as if they're key members of your team, and they're more likely to help you find innovative solutions.

PRICE AND SCOPE

Before you go to the client with a brilliant idea, you should know the price of that idea. That requires scoping the solution thoroughly, now and for the future. This includes planning for contingencies, considering long-term discounts, thinking carefully about how much work the customer will have to devote to this commitment, and balancing the margin. The pricing and scoping process is similar to the process for assessing opportunity, but with better information and heightened focus.

This course of action won't be difficult if the solution involves a standard product or service. But it will take a lot more work and input from your internal partners if you're creating a custom solution for the client. Still, it's a step no one can afford to skip. Unless you've diligently priced and scoped the project before you take it to the customer, the customer will inevitably price it herself. So don't present a solution unless you're ready to have a discussion about price.

"Don't close early — and don't close late," said one rep. "Truly understand what a customer is asking for. Truly understand how you can fulfill the needs of that customer." He also noted that sales reps should never, ever talk about price before they've anticipated and answered every possible question or objection, because failing to do so risks setting an anchor price. We talk more about anchoring prices in Chapter 3. "If price comes up too soon, you are going to price your product at a lower yield than you could have potentially, if you had fulfilled every obligation, every objection, and every need of the organization," the rep said.

Another key element to pricing and scoping is understanding your client's contracting process. You don't want to be sideswiped at the eleventh hour by discovering that your company has a conflicting policy. You should understand how the customer defines a contract, a statement of work, or a letter of intent early in the relationship. Once you know these things, you can tailor your approach to their contracting requirements — which can become another way of finding a solution.

DISCUSSING THE SOLUTION

The final stage is discussing your solution with the client. We use the word *discuss* rather than *present* because at this point, presumably you've filled your operating space the right way. You've asked good questions and developed custom insights; you know the customer's organization and needs and have become a partner and an asset.

"Before you identify any solutions, you've got to build credibility with the customer," said Ron Barczak from Stryker. "They've got to know that you have a lot of ideas, that you know how they do business and how they interact. I do 'state of the union' discussions. I talk about 'This is what you're doing; here's a potential [way] we can help you.' The first and most important thing is building credibility with the customer and then giving them ideas and solutions and working with them to implement them."

Use words that reinforce your partnership. Mention "based on our conversation" or "taking into account your recommendations, this solution seems to be moving us in the right direction." This inclusive language will strengthen the emotional bond you're building with the client.

"Selling, for me, is helping somebody," said Alain Tremblay from Standard Life. "If you help somebody, you will be the first one to contribute [or] to help the firm achieve its objectives. It is not to play a game; it is to make sure that they have what they are looking for exactly. It's how I can help them."

STRENGTHS APPLIED: IDENTIFYING SOLUTIONS

Here are some ideas for identifying solutions using specific talent themes. Now think about your talents and strengths, and come up with some ideas for how you can identify solutions more effectively using your own top five themes.

1. Example: Intellection

    Keep your customers in mind at all times. Every new situation, no matter where or when, can be an opportunity to spark a new thought or insight that will benefit your customer in a way that others miss.

2. Example: Competition

   How can your solutions separate you from the competition? Look closely at the needs of your customers, and discover how your products and services will help them be highly successful. Focus on how your solution is helping your customers compete and win over the long term. When they win, you win. Keep a tally of wins and losses, and make sure there are many more wins than losses on the tally sheet.

3. Example: Positivity

   Always look for ways to bring engaging energy to the situations your clients face. In the most difficult times, they often need help to see the possibilities. You are adept at thinking about possibilities, and your positive energy will help your customers feel hopeful about potential solutions.

4. Example: Developer

   Think about how the solutions you offer can help your clients grow. Ask yourself how you can give your key contacts a chance to discover something new that they didn't realize before. This will provide you with a unique opportunity to connect your solutions to their learning and growth.

5.   Example: Connectedness

How can your solutions have an impact not only on specific problems but also on your client's bigger issues? How could the solutions you provide influence the organization or the community in ways that people don't even realize? Understand that the good you do for your client will come back to you, even if it is not immediately evident.

Chapter 6:
Building Advocacy

THIS CHAPTER'S KEY POINTS

- Like everyone, you need advocates who will say nice things about you and protect the great work you do when you're not around — and when your competitors are. Strong emotional bonds motivate advocates to say the right things. You'll know you've made a big impression when your advocates tell you how they came to your defense.

- Purchasing decisions are rarely made by one person, so having a broad constituency in the client environment is key.

- Your efforts at building advocacy should be authentic and based on your strengths. By using your natural talents, you can turn acquaintances into advocates.

"I was on my way to Silicon Valley to give a presentation to what could have been our biggest client ever," Jerry, a sales professional, told us. "And man, I was prepared: I'd researched that company for weeks. I'd talked with a bunch of their tech guys. I had a beautiful presentation. I'd even developed friendships with the receptionists. I was on point. But then the flight was delayed. I lost my laptop. And when I finally got to San Jose, I couldn't find the place and got to the meeting three hours late with nothing to show them. It was the kind of screw-up you lose your job over."

But Jerry didn't lose his job. He didn't even lose his prospect. The tech guys and a receptionist had convinced the purchasing committee that all the mishaps were just a streak of bad luck. Before he arrived, they had rescheduled the meeting for him and found him a loaner laptop. "I showed up bright and early the next morning, knocked them on their rears, and got the deal. And it's all because a few people who worked there worked for *me*."

All salespeople need advocates who will say nice things about them behind their backs. These champions can provide you with inside information, direct your efforts, connect you with the right people, and — as Jerry's advocates did — even cover for you. Advocates can also provide you with the material you need to build solutions. No matter how diligently you do your research, you can't know everything and everyone. The right advocates already do.

It's not enough to have a single advocate in a customer's organization. Many sales efforts are complex, and they require you to develop and maintain several touchpoints.

"It seems like I have to meet hundreds of people at multiple sites. And I talk to everybody, I mean *everybody*, from the security guard to the cafeteria employees to the building maintenance people to the computer tech people. Everybody," said Steve Sieck from Pfizer, whose top five themes include Woo and Communication.

The best salespeople talk to a host of individuals because they realize that purchasing decisions are rarely made by a single person; most decisions are made by groups. And even those lone decision makers have trusted advisors they listen to who can influence their thinking. That means you need to develop strong relationships with people at every level, and you'll need to get everyone on your side.

For example, if you're selling cars and a couple comes in to buy a minivan, don't dismiss either of them or overlook their children. Involve the entire family. A crucial element in creating advocates is giving everyone a voice. This will keep you from making one of the most ruinous mistakes in sales — assuming the wrong person has the decision-making power and treating others as if they don't matter.

This advice might seem obvious, but even experienced salespeople can make this mistake. When we conducted a focus group for a retail client, female shoppers told us that when they shop for high-end electronics with their husbands, sales reps tend to ignore them. The husbands often do the talking, but these women have equal decision-making power, and retail salespeople discover this at their peril. So don't overlook anyone in the sales process. You'll need everyone to be your advocate, even those who are silent.

Regardless of what you are selling or to whom, advocates are indispensable. Insiders have access to the key decision makers — access that's hard to get early on — and they influence the key decisions. So you should seize every chance to develop champions among customers. The question is: How?

ACQUAINTANCE TO ADVOCATE

There are good ways and bad ways to try to turn acquaintances into advocates. Phoniness or faking rapport with potential advocates is a bad way. A better method is to use your natural talents. Anything else comes across as contrived, and people will see right through it. Your efforts at building advocacy should be authentic. You can get in the door with donuts and decorum, but you keep the door open with dialogue. "Open an opportunity for the customer to talk," said Steve Sieck from Pfizer. "And then listen to what they say. We're building trust here."

You should also do some investigating when you're building your advocacy network. Most successful sales start with an investment in key people. But first, you must determine who those people are. Tools like social maps are great for visual thinkers, and they'll prevent you from overlooking potential advocates. To create a social map, ask yourself: Who are the key decision makers? Who works directly with them? Who doesn't work with them but can influence their decisions? Who can tell me who is missing? Do I know them? Do they have a relationship with me? If not, who can introduce me to them? And remember: You will not always be 100% right, so don't burn any bridges. You can't always know who is influencing whom.

If you're wondering who else should be on your social map, you can always ask your customer for advice. Asking is an underused form of flattery. People like to be asked for their opinions. And you shouldn't stop there. If the customer identifies someone you should know, ask him or her to connect you with that person. This will broaden your reach very quickly.

"I always ask my customer if is there's anybody else I should [talk to]," said Steve Sieck from Pfizer. "They often say, 'You know what? Yeah!' And then I ask, 'Would you call them and help me set up a time to meet with them?'" This is one way Steve makes the most of his Arranger and Maximizer themes. He doesn't settle for one touchpoint. He builds many, and in the process, improves his chances for getting a call or a sale far into the future.

Of course, you must navigate the relationships. "There are a tremendous number of influencers in our business," said John Wells from Interface, who relies on his Maximizer and Individualization themes to get the best out of his advocates and to make sure no business is left on the table. "There are big owners and little owners, account execs, influencers, evaluators. We need to know the people the owners send off to gather the information as well as the people who influence the owners. So mapping all those people [is] really critical in our business." With his awareness of what makes each person tick, John takes what he knows and uses it to his advantage to grow the business.

Most of John's customers are, he said, "made up of multiple individuals, and sometimes we make a mistake by having the relationship with a few, but not with all. And if you're just [talking] with a few, then you feel like you're doing good, but you're missing perhaps the majority of the work. We stress that very heavily — you may be walking past more business than you're trying to build if you don't have relationships throughout the firm."

Many sales reps think that only people with top themes like Woo or Relator can shine in the area of creating advocates, but that's not so. John, who has Maximizer and Includer in his top five themes, said, "I always think there's more to be had from [a] relationship, or that we can [build] some other relationships. . . . It's what gets me out of bed in the morning." His talents help him see how deepening a connection might result in not only his success, but the success of his customer's business. Talents like Woo, Relator, or Includer can help in building relationships and developing advocates, but they're not enough. You need to meet the right people, deepen the relationships, and make sure no one feels used. It is important to rely on more than one talent to solidify champions throughout your customer organization.

FULL COURT PRESS

Even in small organizations, there are many important touchpoints, so it's a good idea to make creating advocates a team effort. You don't have to build embassies all by yourself. You can ask some of your coworkers to get to know key people on the customer's team. Think about how political campaigns work: Only one person runs for office, but candidates often have several dozen staffers creating connections with influential voters. You can apply this approach to building connections with your customers.

And don't forget that a boss or an executive in your own company can be a great advocate too. "I'll be sitting at dinner with a client, and [I] know that we're ready to move into the home stretch. I'll have a senior leader of the organization pick up the phone or get on a plane to say they support me and everything I am trying to do to get their business," said a rep in the hospitality industry. "To hear that from our CEO demonstrates to a customer . . . that the value of their business is very meaningful to us. All bosses have the capacity to do [this] — it's just that my bosses do it all the time."

You might be wondering how this salesperson gets his CEO to hop on a plane on his behalf. It could be explained by one of the rep's top themes, Significance, which inspires him to say, "I deserve this support." Furthermore, the CEO knows that this salesperson is selling top-notch business. But anyone in the company has the potential to increase the value proposition a rep offers.

If your solution involves technology, for example, you might ask someone from IT to call the customer's IT people and offer solutions and insights that only tech types understand. If you encounter obstacles in the accounting or legal departments, who could be a better advocate for you than someone from your own accounting or legal team? The more ways that you can find to mesh your company with the client's, the deeper you'll settle into a partnership.

CHAMPION COACHING

You need your advocates to help manage expectations and overcome others' objections. It's difficult enough to manage expectations; it's harder still to do it by proxy. But when it's time for your advocates to speak up for you, they'll be using their own words, not yours. Teaching an advocate what to say on your behalf is a delicate operation. One salesperson explained it this way: "I've never known how to make someone do what I wanted them to do. So what I've done is make myself someone they want to help. I've used my Empathy to make sure we're on the same wavelength. I've used Connectedness so that my champions are thinking about me when I'm not there. Analytical — that's how you figure out how to make what you're selling good for your champion's career."

This salesperson makes an excellent point: Advocates will be more likely to stand up for you if it benefits them. A real advocate is someone who understands the value you bring and who can argue effectively on your behalf. Your best advocates feel like they have as much skin in the game as you do. So partner with them to craft their message. If you do your work right, your champions will want this coaching from you as much as you want to give it to them. Collaborating with them to figure out the message will give it the most impact.

Regardless of how successfully your advocate influences the boss, that boss is likely to have objections, doubts, or questions. That's part of the game. Be there for your advocate, ready with a response. The best outcome is the opportunity to meet directly with the decision makers. If your advocate sets up a meeting for you and already has the decision makers thinking about your solution, then he or she has done more than enough.

STRENGTHS APPLIED: BUILDING ADVOCACY

Here are some ideas for building advocacy using specific talent themes. Now think about your talents and strengths, and come up with some ideas for how you can build advocacy more effectively using your own top five themes.

1. Example: Discipline

   Put the people you need to stay connected with on your calendar. Make meeting with them a specific task that you can check off your agenda. This will help you stay on target for building and maintaining relationships with people who are important to your success. Consistently checking in with them also helps build trust.

2. Example: Individualization

   Build relationships based on what makes each advocate unique. Seek information that helps you develop an understanding about what is important to your advocates and what they need from you to strengthen your partnership.

3. Example: Harmony

    With internal and external advocates, look for opportunities to help people come together when there is disagreement about or resistance to your solutions or ideas. You will clearly see that these rifts are not productive. Help them see it too. When you are successful, they'll appreciate your willingness to help them work through their issues.

4. Example: Adaptability

    Use your ability to handle shifting priorities to help your clients and your coworkers navigate difficult or confusing times. Your adaptive nature will help you step back and consider alternatives. Ultimately, this can position you as an advisor and help build advocacy.

5. Example: Empathy

    Your ability to pick up on the feelings of others helps you understand when things are going well — or when they're not. You'll have insights long before others who may not be as dialed in to these emotions. Make note of these emotional clues, and see how you can offer assistance. Follow up on hunches that can keep a sale on track.

Chapter 7:
Negotiating and Closing

THIS CHAPTER'S KEY POINTS

- Negotiating and closing shouldn't be negative or one-time events. Instead, they can be a series of value-based encounters that lead a client to find a solution to a problem.

- Anticipating what the customer will need next helps create an ongoing conversation. When you provide clients with value-added insights, closing becomes a natural part of the relationship.

- Your unique talents can contribute to successful negotiating and closing. Using role-playing to perfect your strengths-based technique will help you identify when you are — and are not — using your talents effectively.

- A talent theme that may not seem like it would be advantageous for the process of closing might be your biggest asset.

"I love negotiating," said Geoff Nyheim from Microsoft Online Services. "When it's messed up and everybody's sort of at odds, [I like it] even better. . . . because I think, 'Oh, gosh, I'll fix it.' It's enjoyable, and it's intellectually thrilling. It's interesting and a challenge." Geoff's lucky. Negotiating can be difficult. Some reps feel as if they are putting the client relationship at risk by being confrontational. Others, however, love the process. One account executive told us that negotiating is the best part of his job.

Regardless of how you feel about it, negotiation is an essential part of the sales process. It must be done and done well. And it's easier to negotiate well when you lead with your strengths. People who are strong in Command, for example, are likely to have an edge when it comes to negotiating, if only because being forceful comes naturally to them. People who lead with Self-Assurance are certain they're right, which gives them confidence.

Kelly Matthews, an account manager for Mars Snackfood, views the process of negotiating and closing as a logical part of the conversations she's been having with her clients. "I'm always thinking: What's the next step? What do I need to do now?" she said. "And then I just keep chiseling away at it toward the final objective. I just keep after it. So, for me, closing is more about perseverance." Kelly uses her Achiever and Focus talents to persevere, and her Competition talents make her want to win the business. If you can come up with a solution to a customer's problem (like Kelly does when she figures out the next step), more than half the negotiating is already done.

But no matter what your top five themes are, you can use them to negotiate and close deals in one way or another. For example, you might not think that Learner talents would be useful for closing, but Ron Barczak from Stryker would disagree. "The more information that you can go to the table with," he said, "the more you're going to be able to show them that this is a good scenario for them." Talent themes such as Connectedness, Positivity, or Empathy can help you make an emotional connection with your customers. These themes can be useful in softening up prospects, so when you come to the negotiating table, you are more likely to be seen as an ally than as a rival.

That brings us back to advocates. The best thing in a negotiation is for the decision maker to be your champion. The second best thing is for the decision maker to be surrounded by your advocates. Having people speak for you will come in handy during negotiations; there may be quirks or wrinkles that only an insider would know. For example, a champion can tell you if a letter of intent is as good as gold or just a formality. An insider can tell you if your customer hates hard sells or delights in them. And an advocate can help you know if it's worth your time to continue pursuing the business at all.

If you use your talents effectively to solve problems and develop relationships, you may be able to avoid some of the toughest aspects of negotiating altogether. "If we are accommodating all the issues and if we've hit everything that's important to you as the customer, there's really nothing left to talk about other than to sign the deal," said a hospitality industry salesperson. "At the end of the day, if you've got everything you need, and I've got everything I need, let's go."

This rep is able to orchestrate the process so well because he uses his top talents to the utmost: His Analytical talents help him gather information. His Strategic and Restorative talents help him explore options and find solutions to possible obstacles. His Belief talents infuse value and deeper meaning. And his Significance owns that it can all happen. By the time he asks for the business, it's there for the taking.

Knowing how to use your talents to close takes time, thought, and effort. But what if negotiating makes you uncomfortable and is your big weak spot, and you have a closing meeting in three days? Here's a quick-fix approach: Try role-playing with a colleague or manager who can help you think through all the steps. You should be grounded in every aspect of the deal. After role-playing, when you walk in the room, you will have rehearsed every possible scenario. If surprises make you anxious, you must think them through in advance to minimize your potential for discomfort. Role-playing can help you become desensitized.

Let's break role-playing into steps:

- Ask a colleague or your manager to present you with a variety of possible objections.

- Prepare an answer for every objection, and practice until you can deliver it without sounding defensive or nervous.

- Know where your case is strong, and don't back down.

- Make sure you leave the door open for future business.

WHEN IS A WIN A WIN?

If closing is a nagging limitation that causes problems again and again, you will probably never enjoy it. But you will have to learn how to do it — there's no getting around closing in sales. A college fundraiser we know dreads negotiating and closing. He says he hates conflict, which is what he believes negotiation is. His top five themes — Adaptability, Belief, Harmony, Empathy, and Deliberative — might feel alien to an aggressive hunter. But after working with a strengths performance coach, the fundraiser realized that his talents — especially in Empathy, Harmony, and Belief — got him in doors that others would have difficulty entering.

"I wouldn't do this if I didn't believe so strongly in this institution. And I don't want to spend my life trying to talk to people who don't want to talk to me," he said, reflecting his Belief talents. "So what I've done is use Empathy and Harmony so well that I can talk about my college in a way that makes people understand how they're involved, even if they haven't been on campus in 50 years. They know how important education is, and I can show them how they can be part of some kid's future, just like [our] college was for them. Who would say no to that?"

As you intentionally apply your talents to negotiating and closing, you'll probably become more comfortable with the process. But don't let your improved negotiating ability go to your head. Yes, you may like it more — or hate it less — as you get better at it, and your sales numbers will improve. But remember: The real point of negotiating is to get everyone to a win/win situation; it's not for the sheer fun of landing a big sale.

"There are deals, even very important deals, you just can't do," said Geoff Nyheim from Microsoft Online Services. "We just had a situation that we literally decided to walk away from. That made it virtually impossible for the team to make their quota for the next three years. Yet had we made that sale, the terms and conditions and pricing . . . would have been irresponsible on behalf of our shareholders. Inevitably, given the transparency of information in today's world, the guys up and down Wall Street would have been aware of it, and we would have eroded our market."

There are some deals that aren't worth closing. Sometimes the best alternative is to walk away. Try not to get swept up in the heat of the negotiating moment. If the deal isn't good for both you and the customer, don't do it.

STRENGTHS APPLIED: NEGOTIATING AND CLOSING

Here are some ideas for negotiating and closing using specific talent themes. Now think about your talents and strengths, and come up with some ideas for how you can negotiate and close business more effectively using your own top five themes.

1. Example: Context

    Use past successes to inform present actions as they relate to negotiating and closing. If a client has responded well to a specific approach before, make a note of it and refer to it each time you reach this part of the sales process.

2. Example: Achiever

    Establish the successful close as an objective you need to meet. Whether the sales cycle is long or short, pay attention to where you are in the process. Try breaking down the negotiating and closing parts of the sales process into smaller steps. Then you can check off each step to keep track of all your achievements toward the final goal.

3. Example: Restorative

As part of the negotiating and closing process, try to find ways to solve problems for your customers that your competitors may miss. Look for crucial areas that need to be fixed. Helping them see that you're thinking about how to make things better for them in areas where they are struggling will position you effectively in this part of the sales process.

4. Example: Input

Go into the negotiating and closing process more informed than the client and your competitors. Do your research about the customer's probable objections — and the comparisons they may make between you and the competitors. If you continually show that you have thought through all the issues carefully, it will help you move beyond obstacles.

5. Example: Focus

Keep your eye on the ultimate objective: closing the sale. Use this as your guidepost all through the negotiating process. By focusing on what really matters, you will not be pulled off course by distractions. Your ability to concentrate on your goal will help you stay stable when others are wavering.

Chapter 8:
Serving, Retaining, and Growing

THIS CHAPTER'S KEY POINTS

- You've won the deal. Now it's time to secure the relationship for the long term. Closing the first sale is an opportunity to build a relationship that will last. After the sale, you have the chance every day to show clients why they chose you over your competition.

- Sustaining the client relationship doesn't require a different set of talents than you needed to make the sale. You just need to apply them differently. If you revisit your top five themes frequently, you can see how they can help you stay connected with customers.

- An engaged team of internal partners can help you build enduring connections with your customers.

- The honeymoon period is the perfect time to set up the client relationship for the long term. Asking for what you need to build the right type of partnership and setting clear expectations early will help you overcome issues that arise when the honeymoon is over.

We've used the word *relationship* a lot — and we'll use it a lot more in the chapter on customer engagement. But there's an important aspect of relationships that we haven't yet mentioned: Relationships don't have an end date. A good customer relationship is ongoing. Rita Robison from Jones Lang LaSalle put it bluntly: One-time deals are a waste of time. "One of the worst mistakes you make early in your career is to see each deal as *one* deal. Stay in touch with your clients, and let them be the ones who sell for you," she said.

It's not uncommon to see reps putting all their effort into getting an initial sale, then letting the momentum die once the contract is signed. Yet reps need to recognize that sustaining the relationship can account for tremendous growth in a sales portfolio. If you've applied your talents and strengths to the sale, you have made a great connection. Now, don't blow it — build on it.

"A customer's made a decision to do business with your organization. From that day forward, your job is to reinforce to the customer why they made that decision and why it was a wise one," said one rep. "You have to constantly go to him and reassess the needs of his organization, because they do change. If you're not asking what those needs are, you may miss out on something. Somebody else may come in, uncover that need, and find a way to provide a solution to it. And you may be on the outside looking in one day."

The more we work with salespeople, the more we see that no matter what type of selling they do, they can develop a sustained relationship. For some sales reps, developing the relationship is built right in to the sales process.

Salespeople in the financial sector, for example, usually work with a portfolio of clients they stay close to for years. But all salespeople, even retail clerks, have the potential to develop and deepen relationships.

Peggy, a sales clerk at a department store, has developed a five-year relationship with our colleague Jennifer. When Jennifer's father-in-law died, she needed something to wear to the funeral. And she had her two small sad children with her, neither of whom were in any mood to go shopping. "I knew that shopping trip was going to be miserable and that I'd need help," Jennifer said. "So I marched up to the counter and told the woman there that I needed a black suit. Fast."

Peggy took Jennifer to the biggest dressing room, brought her every black suit the store had in her size, then took the children out. "By the time I'd decided on the suit, Peggy and my two-year-old were playing on the cash register, and my five-year-old was drawing on Peggy's scratch paper." At that point, Jennifer burst into tears, and Peggy handed her a box of tissues and patted her shoulder. "She said she figured that I needed something to wear to a funeral and thought I could use some extra help," Jennifer said. "Since that day, I've bought just about every stitch of clothes I own — and done a lot of my holiday shopping — from Peggy. I don't know what I'm going to do if she ever quits."

So even when you are making what appears to be a one-time sale, it doesn't mean that the relationship is an isolated event. After all, the customer might need only one car, one software package, or one black suit right now. But he may need another one in the future, and he'll be interacting with hundreds of people in between those purchases. Will that customer say good things, bad things, or nothing at all about his salesperson?

Growing an account — getting more business from existing customers — is where the real money is. It's less costly to win more business from current customers than to cultivate new ones. That is why building an expansive relationship and negotiating well is so important. What's more, if you don't grow your accounts — if you don't keep coming up with solutions — your clients may feel that you aren't paying attention or working with their best interests in mind.

ENGAGING YOUR ORGANIZATION

Building on a sale, as opposed to creating one, doesn't require a completely different set of talents. It requires applying your talents differently. "Positivity is way up there in my theme sequence, after Empathy and Relator, and I think that creates deeper relationships," said an energy industry sales rep. "And to be honest, propane is propane. But when I began a start-up from scratch, my first customer at my old company became my first sale at my new one. I called him up and he just said, 'Shoot me some gas.' And I said, 'OK, you want to know the price?' And he said, 'No, I trust you.'" This rep's ability to build and sustain relationships has helped him create an enduring partnership, establishing such solid trust that commodity pricing is removed from the equation.

But you can't sustain a relationship on your own. Selling exists at the intersection of the client's company and the seller's company, and it can affect everyone in both organizations. To build successful long-term relationships with clients, you must get the best from the people in your own company, because those internal partners can make or break your success. There are two ways to go about this: coerce colleagues to help or encourage them to help by enlisting them as partners. Kelly Matthews from Mars Snackfood prefers the latter approach. "Over the years, I've spent a lot of time educating people at our headquarters about [my main client]," she said. "This sharing [includes] what can be accomplished at [the client], their business model, and how we mutually win." In this case, Kelly is doing everything she can to make the relationship better all the time. This is her Maximizer at play.

It seems obvious, but it needs to be said: No one who supports you or the client — from the person who processes the initial order to the person who ships it out the door — should ever feel used. They should feel like partners, not servants. Partners come up with solutions no one else ever thought of, and those solutions can be funneled into the client relationship. What's more, you must be able to show customers that you have an army of talented, dedicated people behind you, each poised to provide solutions.

"If I really had to nail down why I think I've been successful — when I have been; there are plenty of times I've failed — I think it's because I've developed relationships with the people I work with and the people who work for me," said Geoff Nyheim from Microsoft Online Services. "I spend a tremendous amount of time getting to know who they are, why they're that way, and how I can help them. [I want to know] what things I can do to contribute towards them realizing their potential or hopes or dreams. I find out what success looks like for every individual."

At the same time, you must position your clients within your own company. You should show the receptionist, the legal team, the mailroom staff, and operations what the customer means to the organization so they are as willing to go into battle for the client as you are. People work harder for customers they know and care about. "I have an entire organization that I can bring in to help a customer," said a hospitality industry account executive. "It's not just about matching up what he needs with a building that I have. It's about, 'Let's set up my human resource organization to meet with yours. And let us help you benchmark best practices, and here's what we've learned.' So it's about an entire relationship versus just me selling something."

THE HONEYMOON

When we were thinking about the topic of this chapter, we sat down with a highly successful account executive who works with a professional consulting services firm. He has a remarkable track record of selling and growing highly complex, long-term consulting relationships. We thought he might have some great insights — and he did. He said that one of the most critical parts of the sales process is what he refers to as "the honeymoon." He explained, "[It's] the one or two weeks immediately following the formal signing of a contract. The commitment is solid, no one's made a mistake, no one's been fired. This is the worst time to step back, because you'll never have a chance at a totally positive emotional time again."

This sales pro remarked that the honeymoon is the perfect time for clients to find out what to expect from the sales reps — and for the reps to show what they expect and need from clients. It's the ideal time to get the core customer team together with your core internal team. "Bring them together to have dinner and celebrate the new relationship. Introduce everyone, discuss the future, build some personal connections, and make sure the client leaves knowing what everyone needs to be successful in the work," he said.

The honeymoon phase is also the ideal time for you to ask for what you need to get access to the company. And we mean that literally — a key card, an on-site office, or an invitation to the weekly staff meetings — but also access to the people who will be important to the long-term relationship. If you need to know the CEO, this is the time to ask for a meeting or to interview the company's top leaders. Meanwhile, you should be developing more advocates while helping the clients solve their most important problems, ensuring a long-term connection.

This is also a great time to show clients how you deliver value. Perhaps it's a guaranteed turnaround on their requests or a specific level of quality for the product or service. Remember, people love getting more than they think they're paying for, especially from the person who sold it. For example, the sales star we spoke with always brings something extra and unexpected to the table — in his case, an additional on-site consulting day each month that wasn't in the contract.

John Wells from Interface not only brought something extra to the table, he drove it there himself. "I had a very large account, and one particular project of theirs was opening in Mobile, Alabama. But the carpet hadn't been ordered in time," he said. He discovered this when one of the customer's employees called in a panic. She told John that the mayor was coming to the store's grand opening in two days, that the occasion was a very big deal for the city of Mobile, and that the carpet hadn't gotten there yet. John has Belief in his top five themes, and he couldn't leave a customer in trouble. "Luckily, I was within driving distance. So I got a truck, and I drove that carpet down there that night, put the carpet in, and everything went off fine," he said. "This sounds like I'm patting myself on the back, but I will never forget doing this. It was a reasonably good effort on my part, but it more than solidified my relationship with that company forever."

Making the most of the honeymoon phase will help you overcome the issues that will arise when the honeymoon is over, and it will end eventually. The personal emotional framework you establish early on will help you adapt to changing expectations, avoid scope creep, and handle complaints more effectively — all the things that inevitably come up.

But you have to work on the relationship every single day. You must meet with key stakeholders often. Your team needs to stay connected to the client and maintain strong two-way communication. Problems, needs, and successes should stay out in the open. "You have to hear what your customer is telling you," said an energy account executive. "I always want customers to know that we will listen to their problems, their complaints, their good news, their bad news, whatever. We just want to hear it."

He believes that if customers know that the salesperson is listening, they'll find competitors less enticing — even when competitors offer a better price: "Sometimes, to be honest, I'll tell them that's a hell of a deal, they should probably take that. And pretty often — sometimes 10 minutes later, sometimes a month later — they'll call me back and say, 'That great deal I was supposed to get? Well, it didn't turn out that way.' You've got to be able to listen. It's such an important part of the communication."

The best client relationships are based on trust and collaboration, not price. Of course, money will always be an issue. But a salesperson who takes advantage of his or her talents can have real impact on how big of an issue money is. The honeymoon is the time to set up the parameters of the relationship. Base the relationship on partnering, not pricing, and your honeymoon will extend into a very happy marriage.

REFERRALS

One of the best benefits of a growing relationship with a client is that it can lead to referrals, which are gold for salespeople. As you'll see in the chapter on customer engagement, there's a crucial difference between satisfied customers and engaged customers. Satisfied customers will say they'll recommend you, and maybe they will. But a recommendation isn't the same thing as a passionate referral. You don't want your clients just saying that you're a good person with a good product at a good price. You want your clients declaring to their peers that you're the only person they'll do business with.

Asking for referrals is sometimes easier for people with certain top talent themes — like Self-Assurance, Command, Strategic, Maximizer, or Activator — than it is for others. It can be tougher for those with less blatantly assertive talents or for those who build their client relationships on friendship. For these people, asking for referrals may feel pushy. If so, they might be looking at referrals the wrong way. When a client gives a referral, he's offering a testimony to the value you and your organization bring to his business. A customer who is willing to refer you and your organization is seizing an opportunity to promote a smart decision he made in selecting you. You shouldn't let clients miss opportunities to make themselves look good. And often, engaged customers will volunteer recommendations without being asked.

Even if asking for referrals makes you ill at ease, you should ask anyway. "I never felt comfortable asking for referrals because it's like asking someone to stump for you," one salesperson told us. "[It's] like asking your girlfriend if she knows any single women. But when we remodeled our house, we hired a contractor who was fantastic. I told him he ought to put our kitchen on his website, and I told everybody about this guy — and I realized I was doing for him what I'm uncomfortable doing in my own job." That salesperson is now an ace at getting referrals.

STRENGTHS APPLIED: SERVING, RETAINING, AND GROWING

Here are some ideas for serving, retaining, and growing customers using specific talent themes. Now think about your talents and strengths, and come up with some ideas for how you can serve, retain, and grow your customers more effectively using your own top five themes.

1. Example: Relator

    Look at all aspects of your client relationships, and understand that your connection with customers can go beyond business as usual. Take the time to work as closely as possible with clients so that you become a trusted advisor to them. Meaningful bonds with clients build sustainable relationships that create long-term growth. Capitalize on your ability to establish these types of connections with your customers.

2. Example: Futuristic

    Where do we go from here? What lies beyond the
    horizon for your business needs? These are the
    kinds of questions you want to ask your customers.
    Understand their growth strategies and what you
    can do to be a part of that future. Start with a "state
    of the union" to ensure that you're meeting their
    current needs. Use this as a building block to devise
    a strategy *with* them to make sure that you will
    be meeting their future needs. Become embedded
    in their vision, and retention is likely to be a
    natural byproduct.

3. Example: Competition

    Keep an eye on your competitors. Closing the deal
    over the competition is like making an important
    point in a ball game: The real game continues
    as long as there is a chance that you could lose.
    Lots of games have been won by teams that were
    behind. So establish your own personal contests to
    set yourself apart from the competitors. Beat them
    even when they don't realize they're in the game.
    Make sure you don't fall into the trap of believing
    you've won. Sales is a continuing competition.
    Keeping and growing business is key to long-term
    performance. Stay in it for the long haul. You don't
    want to take the existing wins for granted while
    pursuing the next victory.

4. Example: Communication

    Stay in touch with your customers. Regularly share ideas and information that you think will help them. Ask questions about how their business is doing and if you and your organization are meeting and surpassing expectations. These ongoing interactions keep you connected and help clients see you as a valuable partner. Use communication as a way to reinforce your value. Use stories of real situations to help your customers see the benefits of working with you.

5. Example: Arranger

    Try to find ways to multiply your benefits throughout the customer organization. Your ability to juggle and multitask will allow you to create energy around the work you do in the client organization. Look for ways to keep your partnership dynamic. Connect people and ideas. Use your ability to deal with multiple things simultaneously to help your clients when they seem overwhelmed. Be the person who knows all the moving parts and pieces.

Chapter 9:
Team Sales

THIS CHAPTER'S KEY POINTS

- Sales teams are most effective when the product or service requires a broad knowledge base, when the clients have many decision makers, and when the geographical territory is large.

- Understanding the talents of your team members — knowing who does what well — is crucial. Members of the most successful teams have a heightened awareness of how they are alike and how they are different.

- The best teams are carefully designed and are characterized by complementary strengths, a common mission, fairness, trust, acceptance, forgiveness, communicating, and unselfishness.

- Communication is key to performance.

Traditionally, sales has been thought of as a single-player game, and it may continue to be in your company. But a team sales model is becoming more common. Some customers expect a great deal of attention and know-how from their suppliers — more than a single rep can handle. In response, many companies have found success by creating teams of experts to support their clients. Different decision makers also have different needs and styles, and individual salespeople cannot possibly be a fit with all the buyers they encounter.

This is the situation that Pfizer Oncology encountered, and they found a solution in team selling. Pfizer Oncology believed that deep product expertise on Pfizer's significantly expanded product portfolio was too much for any one rep. So they divided the portfolio between two reps working in the same territory. Both salespeople, each offering specialized knowledge, called on the same doctors. The approach worked so well that four years later, Pfizer Oncology completely adopted a "dyad" model, in which a pair of seasoned sales reps share the exact same goals and variable-comp plans. Most of the reps were promoted into this role in one of the most elite sales organizations at Pfizer. We conducted a focus group with Mike Scouvart's Mid-Atlantic sales region to find out why the team selling approach worked so well.

The first thing we noticed was the emphasis that the account executives put on talents and strengths. They're well aware that each member of the dyad has a different set of talents and how those talents work together. "Oftentimes we complement one another," said one of the representatives. "We have different ideas, look at things differently, and connect to different people. When we come together, we strengthen our ideas and our focus."

It took a while to get to that point, however. When team member talents aren't identified, cultivated, understood, or applied properly, teams aren't as effective. What's more, it can take some time to calibrate talents, as Pfizer Oncology's team members discovered. "We had some very rough days at first, and I think it was because my partner and I are very different people," said one of the reps. "We think differently. We process things differently. We do have the same work ethic, which is what holds us together. But we did not respect each other the way that we needed to make our relationship work. And we had conversations on the phone after work that were just knock-down, drag-out fights."

Pfizer Oncology is a strengths-based organization, however, so the pairs didn't pit their talents against each other for long. With some insights and help from a strengths performance coach, the salespeople learned how to apply the best of themselves in tandem. "We've come to know one another's strengths very well," one of the account executives said. "This [awareness] has helped us build an incredible trust, and because of that and playing to our individual strengths, we know we can work out whatever is put in front of us."

Soon, the reps benefited from a strengths-savvy team approach, and so did their customers. Sales styles differ, but so do buying styles. In the complex field of oncology, the needs of physicians and their patients can be extraordinarily different. A well-designed team can offer more talents, which makes meshing with clients and meeting their needs smoother and more efficient.

PRECISION DESIGN

Team-based selling can be exceptionally effective — but it can also drive people crazy. Whether it does or not depends on how the teams are formed. In their book *Power of 2*, Rodd Wagner and Gale Muller examined what makes good partnerships work. They discovered that the most successful and effective partnerships are characterized by complementary strengths, a common mission, fairness (so consider pay carefully), trust, acceptance, forgiveness, communicating, and unselfishness. Managers can help ensure team sales success by partnering people with these key attributes in mind, then supporting them.

StrengthsFinder is a good resource for pairing team members based on complementary strengths. Two people with strong Competition might butt heads, for example, but if they also lead with talents like Communication and Harmony, they can work around conflicts. Having two people who lead with Analytical on a team is great for finding solutions, but Analytical plus Discipline plus Empathy plays to different parts of the sales process and helps a team stay focused on information, attentive to details, and understanding of differing points of view. "We're really relying on each other here," said Dana Fiser, vice president of corporate operations at Jenny Craig. "We have to trust each other in a team because we're very vested in working with each other."

A mix of talents and strengths can help meet the customer's needs too. A high-octane client may initially respond well to a sales team with strong Command, Competition, or Self-Assurance talents. But sooner or later, a contract will need to be negotiated. A team that also brings Harmony, Relator, or Connectedness talents can use finesse when it's needed.

And we can't overemphasize the value of communication, as Wagner and Muller noted in their book. Team members need to talk — constantly. They must openly own their talents and their limitations and discuss where each can contribute the most and where each might need help. One of the things they need to communicate — and perhaps one of the hardest to discuss — is what each team member likes and dislikes about working with the other. Disagreements between people are often due to differences in their talents, but differences can be a source of high performance. That's why constant communication is vital.

The Pfizer dyads communicate about their clients, their strengths, their demands, and their victories as many as four times every day, one rep told us. They talk in person, on the phone, via text messaging and e-mail — whatever's handy. "Success depends on mutual respect of each other," said one of the Pfizer reps. "A lot of people have differences, and if they don't respect their differences, they don't ever get a chance to use and take advantage of them. What we've been able to do as a team is leverage the strengths of two extremely different people. We recognize that, we'll be the first to tell you. But we're a team that has been able to take the best of both of us and respect that and make the most of it."

STRENGTHS APPLIED: TEAM SALES

Here are some ideas for how to be more effective at team sales using specific talent themes. Now think about your talents and strengths, and come up with some ideas for how you can be more effective at team sales using your own top five themes.

1. Example: Empathy

    The dynamics of a team can often be confusing. Use your ability to pick up on the emotions that occur within the team to help individuals better understand one another and why they may be feeling the way they do. You can help clarify relationships for team members.

2. Example: Discipline

    Offer your organizational talents to the team. Others may not be as effective at tracking and organizing as you are, so they will benefit from your ability to make sense of the workflow and the details of how things should progress. Don't impose your approach on others, but help them make sense of the work and what is most important to selling and serving the team's customers.

3. Example: Woo

    You will connect quickly with other members of the team. Use this talent to bring the team together. Your natural social abilities will energize team relationships. This will help build synergy and can make team selling more fun.

4. Example: Ideation

    Infuse the team with your new ideas and thinking. Offer insights that are beyond the norm. Challenge your team to look for innovative ways to build cohesion while providing exemplary service to your customers. Your creativity can help keep things fresh and interesting while the team creates better solutions for your customers.

5. Example: Strategic

    Help your team look for alternatives and multiple pathways to success. By thinking about various solutions, you will expand the team's ability to think beyond Plan A, just in case the client has other needs. Encourage team members to bounce these alternative strategies off one another to create more robust client solutions.

Chapter 10:
Engaging Your Customers

THIS CHAPTER'S KEY POINTS

- Negative and directive relationships with customers make you a vendor, not a partner. By developing expansive relationships, you can become a trusted partner to your customers.

- Expansive customer relationships are formed by building on Confidence, Integrity, Pride, and Passion.

- Making the most of your unique talents enables you to more efficiently build expansive customer partnerships that last.

We've mentioned customer engagement before, and many companies think they have a handle on it. While most businesses probably have some sort of customer satisfaction program, frankly, we don't think they do much good. Customer satisfaction is *not* the same thing as customer engagement. Satisfaction might be a necessary foundation for building strong customer relationships, but it doesn't predict future customer behavior — or an organization's financial performance — very well.

Our research shows that customers who are extremely satisfied fall into two groups: those who are emotionally satisfied and those who are rationally satisfied. Emotionally satisfied customers have a strong emotional attachment to your organization or its products and services; rationally satisfied customers don't. Customers who are emotionally satisfied deliver significant value to an organization. They buy more products and spend more for those products; they return to your business more often, and they stay your customers longer. Rationally satisfied customers, in contrast, don't behave any differently from customers who are dissatisfied.

The hard fact is that soft stuff, like emotions, counts with customers. Simon Cooper, former president and CEO of The Ritz-Carlton Hotel Company, put it perfectly: "When it comes to customers, feelings are facts." We need to recognize that in addition to a rational sales environment, we also live and work in an emotional one. When it comes to engaging customers, meeting their emotional requirements may be just as important as meeting their rational needs.

"My best sale probably happened because they knew I was going to stand by what I said," said John Wells from Interface. It is easy to see John's Belief and Individualization talents in action. His Belief establishes a true sense of value, and his Individualization helps him focus on customers' unique needs. "My personal integrity and the relationship were the things that they trusted. Clearly, the product had to meet their needs, but I think that they were looking for a relationship too." That relationship is called customer engagement.

THE EMOTIONS OF CUSTOMER ENGAGEMENT

In addition to rational components, customer engagement is built on a hierarchy of four emotional needs:

- The first one, the foundation, is a sense of *Confidence* that you and your company can be trusted to deliver on your promises, day in and day out.

- The second dimension is *Integrity* — customers' belief that you'll treat them fairly and resolve their problems quickly.

- The third dimension is *Pride* in being associated with your company. Customers like to feel good about the decisions they make and to see themselves as capable and competent. A company that makes its customers feel that way generates a strong positive association in their hearts and minds.

- The fourth level is *Passion*. Passionate customers describe their relationship with you as irreplaceable and a perfect fit for their needs — they just couldn't do without you. Passionate customers are rare. Only 18% of customers say they feel passionate about a brand. But they are customers for life, and they're your best advocates.

When customers feel that those emotional needs are met every time they do business with you, they are much likelier to become emotionally engaged with your company. "It's about trust, loyalty, respect, the extent to which people see you as a peer," said Geoff Nyheim from Microsoft Online Services. "Whoever you're selling to, do they see your company as people they like, trust, respect? Do you care enough to know their business, their people, their politics, their governance model, their comp plan? And is there a genuineness?"

You're probably highly engaged with one or two companies or brands. What product or service couldn't you live without? What did that business — and the people who work there — do to engage you? No doubt you feel entirely secure dealing with them. You know they will back up what they promise. You're proud of the products or services they provide, and you feel that they're a perfect fit for who you are. "I am totally addicted to Starbucks," a colleague mentioned. "I like everything they serve and everyone who works there. I get coffee there every day before work, and it's where I hang out on weekend mornings. If Starbucks stopped selling coffee, I'd stop drinking coffee." *That's* an engaged customer.

What is your company doing to create customers who are this engaged? What can you do to increase your customers' feelings of Confidence, Integrity, Pride, and Passion? What's more, why should you care? You should care because engaged customers deliver far more value to you and your company than satisfied ones. Fully engaged customers — those with a strong emotional connection —

deliver a 23% premium over average customers in terms of share of wallet, profitability, revenue, and relationship growth. Customers who are actively disengaged — those who have no emotional connection to your organization — represent a 13% discount. And business units with customer engagement levels that are in the top 25% on Gallup's customer engagement measure tend to outperform all other units in their organization on measures of profit contribution, sales, and growth by a ratio of two to one.

Satisfied customers, on the other hand, are no more loyal than dissatisfied ones and don't spend as much as engaged customers. When Gallup studied customer engagement at a large U.S. retail bank, we found that the attrition rate among dissatisfied customers was 5.8% — scarcely different from the 6% attrition rate of satisfied customers — while it was only 3.8% for customers who were emotionally engaged. And in one study at a credit card company, Gallup found that emotionally satisfied customers increased spending by 67% over a 12-month period, while rationally satisfied customers upped their purchases by 8%.

ENGAGING YOUR CUSTOMERS

Unfortunately, there's no magic formula for engaging customers. And it encompasses every interaction a customer has with your company, so you can't do it alone. Even if you are the world's most engaging salesperson, you can't control every aspect of the design, manufacturing, distribution, and customer service processes. All those things have an impact on whether or not your customer feels that your product or service has integrity and is something to be confident in, proud of, and passionate about.

But there are significant elements of engagement that are within a salesperson's control. The primary one is the emotional connection a customer feels with the company. Gallup did a study of the brain activity of highly engaged customers compared to less engaged customers using an fMRI machine. When we analyzed the results, we found that when customers thought about their most beloved brands — the ones they felt most passionately about — the emotional centers of their brains lit up. One of the biggest effects was in the parts of the brain that recognize faces. In other words, when customers were thinking about the companies they were most passionate about, they recalled images of the people they interacted with there. This strongly suggests that the human connection is a powerful avenue to engagement and underscores each employee's role in building customer engagement in every employee-customer encounter.

So you should do whatever you can to connect with your customers by building strong relationships grounded in trust and fairness — relationships that make your customers feel capable, competent, and smart — and ultimately make them feel that you and your company cannot be replaced. How you make that human connection depends on your talents and strengths. If you don't connect with others through wit and easy conversation, for example, you shouldn't try to start now. You'll come across as insincere and awkward. Instead, you should connect with customers in your own way.

Mark sells laboratory equipment, and he leads with Competition, Learner, and Discipline. Those with strong Competition want to outperform their peers and counterparts in other organizations. Learners tend to love knowledge and discovery, and the Discipline theme pushes people to build structure in their lives. Those strengths make driven, inquisitive, organized Mark a pretty good fit for his job. But they don't make him outgoing. Mark's "getting to know you" tactics consisted of fly-by chats. He was so concerned with the numbers and staying on schedule that he missed opportunities to connect with his customers, which could make his relationships seem shallow and tentative. Most customers need more connection than that. With that in mind, Mark marshaled his talents to work around his weakness.

He started by orienting his Competition toward long-term rather than short-term wins. That wasn't so hard. The hard part was reapplying his Learner theme; Mark thought he *did* know his customers. He knew that the customer in Yakima had a near-antique centrifuge. He knew that the customer in Boise City's hydrocollator was the best on the market. He knew that the phlebotomist in Seattle was propping up her draw chair with folded-up scrap paper. What more could there be to know?

It wasn't until he met with a strengths performance coach that Mark realized he didn't know his customers at all —

he just knew their labs. What Mark needed to do was focus his Learner on the people, not the products. Mark's coach told him to use himself as a practice model, so he sat down and thought about what his closest friends knew about him: his likes, dislikes, information about his kids, even his favorite baseball team. He used what he learned to come up with questions to ask his customers. He didn't stop inquiring about their pulse oximeters, but he also started asking about their families, their vacations, and their lives.

Meanwhile, Mark's Discipline was pushing him to systematize what he learned. He started a file about each of his customers. He noted their equipment needs, but he also jotted down that Maryanne in Tacoma hates oranges and that Ang in Salt Lake is a Packers fan. He even built a schedule in his files to make sure he was touching base with every customer at least twice a month — no more fly-bys, no more near anonymity among people he'd "known" for years.

Sound complicated? It isn't. It took Mark less than two hours to come up with his system, and it uses his natural tendencies to get things moving and keep him on track. It might sound trivial or mundane to some. That's fine. You might not want or need to do what Mark did — but you *can* connect with customers in your own way.

To help, we've provided you with a customer interview made up of nine questions. (See sidebar "Customer Interview") You may want to sit down and ask a customer all nine questions, or you might want to slip one or two into a conversation. Either way, it's a good way to begin building your relationships. Of course, many good salespeople already do this without thinking about it. But *deliberately* coordinating strengths and working on engagement — yours and the customers' — makes a big difference in performance.

CUSTOMER INTERVIEW

1. Overall, what things are working well as a result of our partnership?

2. What elements of this relationship are helping us build solid results together?

3. Is there anything that is *not* going as well as it should be?

4. What could we change to correct this?

5. Are you dealing with any issues right now that I could help you work through to improve your business?

6. Is there any information or education you need that you are not able to get?

7. If you could change one thing about how we are working together, what would it be?

8. What would you *never* change about the way we work together?

9. Is there anything else that would help us build an even stronger working relationship?

A VENDOR NO MORE

Customers who are not engaged, or even disengaged, see you as a vendor. Vendors provide needed goods and services at a fair price. When satisfaction with those offerings diminishes or the perception of a good price/ value relationship changes, that vendor relationship is in jeopardy. Customers are constantly haggling and quick to complain, and the relationships are rarely win/win. This is an example of a negative relationship.

Negative relationships are price relationships, and they have little to do with engagement. "They're 'hope' orders," said Ron Barczak from Stryker. "You give them the information, and then you hope you get the deal." If you're in a negative relationship, you're only as good as your price. "You get the sale because you have quoted the lowest price," said one rep. "And you will have one moment of enjoyment, and that is the moment you get the business. But from that moment forward, all you do is worry about when you're going to lose the business."

Some signs of a negative relationship are:

- Your customer doesn't need or want to meet with you. You conduct most of the business on the phone, or worse yet, via e-mail, and often through a gatekeeper.

- Your customer is always badgering you for a discount.

- Your customer frequently indicates that he or she is shopping around.

- Your customer pits you against salespeople from other companies.

- You don't know anything about your customer or your customer's business other than the aspect that concerns your product or service.

- Your customer doesn't trust you.

- You think more about the next sale than about the customer's current situation.

- You think a lot more about how the sale will benefit you rather than how it will benefit your customer.

Let's use car sales as an example of a price-based, negative relationship. People who don't have an existing relationship with an automotive salesperson typically walk onto a car lot with one thing in mind: price. The salespeople know that if they offer the cheapest price, they'll sell cars. And since most of them are commissioned to sell cars, not engage customers, the negotiations are focused on price. So they try to make money any way they can — selling things like warranties, floor mats, and options. They make the process cumbersome, and they make the customer wait longer than necessary because they figure if they can't make the customers pay, they'll make them "pay." Consumer loyalty to dealers is notoriously low as a result, even when customer satisfaction scores are high.

Directive relationships are better than negative relationships, but not much. In directive relationships, salespeople make the sales process bearable rather than terrible. Customers feel like the salesperson is doing just enough to get by, but no more.

These are some indicators of a directive relationship:

- You know just enough to answer your customer's basic questions.

- You tend to give all customers the same advice, and it's based on what you know about your business rather than what you know about theirs.

- Customers would describe their encounter with you as "fine" or "nothing special."

- You think more about the next sale than your current situation.

- You think a lot more about how the situation can benefit you rather than how it will benefit your customer.

Let's use car sales as our example again. Salespeople in directive relationships will try to get through the process as fast as they can so they can get to the next sale (or their coffee break). The process isn't as aggressive, but it's not centered on the customer either. Reps still try to upsell, but they're more likely to ask the customer questions and offer information. They may point out a few things that the customer didn't consider when comparing pricing, such as financing options or rebates. Ultimately, though, their suggestions will be self-serving, and the customer won't leave feeling compelled to shop there again — or to recommend the car lot.

Expansive relationships are the sweet spot of sales, and all salespeople should be striving for this type of customer relationship. Price is no longer the main issue. Your customer considers you a partner, and you start to act like one.

This is how to tell if you're in an expansive relationship:

- You know all the key people in the customer's business, including the support staff and the operations team. They know and like you too.

- You work with your own product development people to find solutions for each client.

- In times of trouble, your customer calls you. In times of success, your customer calls you.

- You use the word "we" when talking about that client, no matter whom you're talking to.

- You know when and where your customer is having trouble, and you spend a lot of time coming up with ways to help.

- You would genuinely grieve if you lost the client, and your client feels the same way about you.

Let's go to back to car sales, but this time for a positive example that Kevin, a car buyer, related to us. "When we had the second baby, my wife said we had to have a minivan," Kevin said. "So we walked on to the lot, and we were ready to buy if we could get the price we wanted. To be honest, I just wanted to get it over with. But we were barely inside the door when Joyce came up."

Kevin said that ordinarily, he'd feel pressured by that, because he likes to look around awhile before the sales pitch. But Joyce didn't begin with a sales pitch; instead, she started by asking questions about his family's needs. "I've never enjoyed buying cars, so I unloaded — told her everything we learned about the minivan we wanted, starting with what we were willing to pay," Kevin said. Joyce told him that their numbers were right on and that their research was solid. "But she didn't sell me the car I wanted at the price I named just so I'd buy the thing and leave. She asked us what the primary purpose of the car would be, and we said it was to haul the kids around," Kevin said.

Joyce then asked if they had considered a used vehicle. "I said that we hadn't, because I wanted the kids and my wife to be safe, and I don't trust used vehicles that much," Kevin said. "Joyce understood that. She said she wasn't going to make a living by selling people chancy cars." But the car lot had some highly reliable, low-mileage vehicles that had gone through 100-point inspections — and one in particular was rated much higher in all safety and durability categories than the new minivan Kevin and his wife were considering. "We wound up saving money on a much safer vehicle than the one we originally thought we wanted."

"Joyce didn't have to do that. She'd have made a bigger commission if she'd sold us the one we originally wanted," Kevin said. "She was really trying to figure out how to help us. She wasn't just hoping to get us to spend more money. She was trying to help us get the right car for our needs. Now, I'm not going to drive a minivan. But I do need to get a family of four in my car too." Kevin drives a 2008 Mustang, so he'll almost certainly need a different car. "And you can bet I'll be calling Joyce," he said.

That's an expansive encounter, the first step toward an expansive relationship. If Joyce continues down this path, Kevin will continue to do business with her, and he'll encourage his friends to do the same. And Joyce will be taking a lot of business away from sales reps who are driving away customers with negative and directive encounters.

STRENGTHS APPLIED: ENGAGING YOUR CUSTOMERS

Here are some ideas for engaging your customers using specific talent themes. Now think about your talents and strengths, and come up with some ideas for how you can engage your customers more effectively using your own top five themes.

1. Example: Communication

    Look for ways to connect the dots between the information you have and how it will benefit your customers. Share this information and stories about things that are important to your customers as a way to continue to deepen your connection with them.

2. Example: Responsibility

    Use your Responsibility talents to demonstrate to your customers that you are committed to your partnership with them. Show them that no matter how long you have worked together, you do not take the relationship lightly and you will follow through on your promises to them.

3. Example: Focus

    Set short-term and long-term objectives that benefit you and your customers. Use these objectives as guides for helping your relationship grow in a positive and productive direction. Tie numbers and measures to these targets whenever possible to help you know when you have achieved the goal.

4. Example: Individualization

    Take the time to truly understand your customers. Find out what makes them unique. What are their hobbies and special interests? What are their strengths? What do you know about their families and their challenges at work? They are people. Get to know them.

5. Example: Activator

    Differentiate yourself through your actions. What are you doing that is different and meaningful to your customers? How is it that your quick actions separate you from the pack? Act, but make sure you are acting in a way that creates expansive relationships with your customers.

Chapter 11:
Engaging Yourself

THIS CHAPTER'S KEY POINTS

- A strengths-based approach creates stronger employee engagement. Linking your strengths to the work you do each day will increase your chances of being engaged.

- There are 12 elements of employee engagement. Knowing and understanding each of them is key to managing your engagement.

- Higher levels of employee engagement lead to higher levels of performance and stronger, more positive relationships with customers.

When Carl's company decided to close its Richmond, Virginia office, it offered everyone there a job at its Roanoke facility. Many of the Richmond folks quit, but not Carl. Even though it meant pulling his kids out of school, talking his wife into quitting her job, and incurring substantial moving costs in a bad housing market, Carl never considered leaving the company. "This company has been good to me," he said during the contentious meeting the firm held to discuss the shutdown. "And I think it's my turn to stand up for it." Carl, by the way, is a janitor — and a highly engaged employee.

If you're using your innate talents on the job, so much so that you're building them into strengths, you're likely to be an engaged employee. But employee engagement is more than liking a job, just as customer engagement is more than being satisfied with a product, service, or business. Employee engagement is an emotional and psychological bond to your work and your employer. It's "an intrinsic desire and passion for excellence. Engaged employees want their organization to succeed because they feel connected emotionally, socially, and even spiritually to its mission, vision, and purpose," wrote John Fleming and Jim Asplund in *Human Sigma: Managing the Employee-Customer Encounter.*

ENGAGEMENT AT WORK

When you are using your strengths, work feels effortless, pressure seems manageable, and you're likely to find greater reward in what you do. When you are doing what you're really good at, it feels easy and natural. Experiencing this personal satisfaction can be addictive — in a good way. It propels you to be better, reach higher, and do more than you thought you could. If you can get that feeling at work, you'll develop a psychological attachment to your job. A workplace that can sustain this feeling lets you make the most of your talents and rewards you with recognition and further opportunities. When all these pieces fall into place, you are likely to find yourself on the track to engagement. When that happens, there is no better way to make a living.

But when the workplace doesn't foster that emotional connection, it is harder to be engaged. "Last year, my company wanted us to work from home. It was OK, but I realized that being that independent is something that I really have a problem with," said a rep whose top themes include Woo. "Connecting over the phone is not the same as being there. I became a bit less engaged and it definitely [affected] my performance and my attitude." Because of this rep's strong Woo talents, working alone disrupted his emotional connection to his job. And that emotional connection has a profound impact on employee engagement.

For companies, engagement is particularly valuable because engaged workers are more productive and sell more. Many companies say their most important assets are their employees, but that's not true. Their most important assets are their *engaged* employees.

Employee engagement is good for your organization, but it's also good for you. Gallup's research shows that the more engaged you are, the more you sell. Beyond that, the research shows strong linkages between higher engagement and better health. Employees with increased levels of engagement have decreases in cholesterol and triglyceride levels. And engaged employees are about half as likely to have been diagnosed with clinical depression — and are 40% less likely to have been diagnosed with anxiety — compared to workers who are actively disengaged. They also have better quality of life ratings: 60% of those who are engaged with their work say they experience thriving wellbeing; in contrast, only 28% of actively disengaged workers experience thriving wellbeing. Furthermore, Gallup has found an important overlap between strengths and engagement: The more you can use your strengths, the more likely you are to be engaged.

THE HEART OF EMPLOYEE ENGAGEMENT

Gallup has studied employee engagement for decades. We've asked millions of employees hundreds of different questions to find the ones that consistently differentiated top-performing workgroups from lower performing ones. After a comprehensive review, 12 elements emerged as those that had the most consistent linkages to performance — the Q^{12}. These items also did the best job of measuring how well companies were meeting employees' core requirements on the job.

These are the 12 items that get at the heart of employee engagement:

1. I know what is expected of me at work.

2. I have the materials and equipment I need to do my work right.

3. At work, I have the opportunity to do what I do best every day.

4. In the last seven days, I have received recognition or praise for doing good work.

5. My supervisor, or someone at work, seems to care about me as a person.

6. There is someone at work who encourages my development.

7. At work, my opinions seem to count.

8. The mission or purpose of my company makes me feel my job is important.

9. My associates or fellow employees are committed to doing quality work.

10. I have a best friend at work.

11. In the last six months, someone at work has talked to me about my progress.

12. This last year, I have had opportunities at work to learn and grow.

When Gallup conducts an employee engagement assessment, employees' responses to the Q^{12} items enable Gallup to determine how effective an organization's managers and employees are at creating engagement. So what do engagement numbers tell managers? Employees' responses to these items give managers insights into how well the team's needs are being met. The results show which needs are being met and where the opportunities for improvement are. They also help managers understand what needs aren't being met so they can work with employees to fix the problems and increase engagement. They provide a springboard for discussion about how to improve the work environment at the local level.

YOUR ENGAGEMENT

A company's or a sales team's engagement might seem irrelevant to many salespeople because they consider themselves autonomous. Most reps spend much of their time alone, are paid on commission, and are ultimately responsible for managing the client relationship. That kind of independence can mask the importance of engaging with a team or a manager. While some people might like to be left alone, no one wants to be ignored. We can all benefit from attention, investment, and at least occasional partnership. So how do you get engaged with your job? Big paychecks, impressive titles, and fancy offices won't do it, at least not for the long term.

Managers have a tremendous amount of influence over employee engagement. Gallup research has found that people don't leave companies so much as they leave managers, and a great manager is the surest route to outstanding team and individual performance. But some managers don't manage the way individuals want or need to be supervised — they manage the way they were taught, or the way they themselves prefer to be managed. What does that mean to you? To become engaged in your work and get the most out of your talents, you may need to take ownership of your own engagement. And that may mean talking with your boss about how he or she can best support you.

YOUR RELATIONSHIP WITH YOUR BOSS

Some of us have incredibly talented bosses who were born to be managers. "The best bosses give you support, collaboration, partnership," said a senior vice president of sales and marketing at a hospitality company. "One of my first directors of marketing took a real interest in making sure that everything I did moved me closer to a deal. And there's nothing that he wouldn't do to help me with it. I remember one day he came in my office and said, 'Let's go take a walk.' So we went outside and just walked around the parking lot. And he made me talk through where I was with this major deal that we were working on. It was just the most encouraging, motivating dialogue that I've had with a boss. And, you know, when it finally did go down, when we got the sale, he was happier for me than I was."

If you have a manager like that, count your blessings and schedule a meeting to discuss your strengths. These kinds of managers love learning about your talents because they love discovering better ways to maximize individual abilities. They really want to see their people succeed. If you don't have that kind of manager, think about the best way to begin a conversation with your manager about applying your strengths to selling. One way to do this is by using your past success to bolster your credibility.

Let's consider Gary, a sales rep for a food company. "My boss would throw me out of his office if I started spouting off about something he didn't think was worth his time, which is basically anything he believes in and nothing else," Gary said. "So I got my numbers for the past 18 months and compared them to my sales notes." Gary was able to show a clear link between his sales activities and his commission, which proved that the more time he spent in face-to-face meetings, the better he did. "I had it in black and white that to get the outcomes he wants, I have to get in front of clients," Gary said. And it's easy to see why. Gary's top five themes all have to do with relating to people. After reviewing the numbers, Gary's boss agreed to let him do less cold calling and more road work because it gets them what they both want — more sales.

Remember, all your talents are important to your success, even when you don't see a direct connection between your talents and your results. So when you go to your manager with a list of your talents and a list of outcomes, don't dismiss talents that may not seem relevant. For example, salespeople with a lot of Discipline are likely to break goals into short-term benchmarks and tasks. Connecting those tasks with the manager's expectations can help prevent confusion about priorities. If you have Restorative in your top five themes, ask your manager if there is anyone on the team who has a challenge and needs help. When having discussions with your manager, use your successes as supporting evidence. What you want is the opportunity to use your strengths to improve your sales and your engagement. It's a win/win for you and your organization.

As you're preparing for your talk with your manager, here are some great questions to consider asking:

- What do you consider to be the most important aspects of my job?

- Thinking about those critical aspects, what do you think I do really well? Where do you think I excel?

- What strengths do you see me using in those areas where I'm excelling?

- For areas where I may not be excelling, how might we partner more effectively to make sure I'm meeting expectations?

- What other strengths do I have that I can take advantage of?

Here's a good example of how to do this: Paul works for a major U.S.-based contracting company in Asia. Among his top five themes are Focus and Responsibility. Paul's boss wasn't very clear about objectives, and this ambiguity was becoming increasingly frustrating. So Paul took charge and decided that getting clarity about his job was his responsibility. He asked for a meeting with his manager.

First, they discussed his responsibilities as a salesperson. Paul's boss started by telling him that he was doing great work and that he should keep plugging away. "Keep doing what you are doing, but do more of it," was his boss' typical line. But this time, Paul tried a new approach to get the clarity he needed. He broke down his job into specific categories, and one by one, he walked his boss through them.

To help Paul maximize his time, together they negotiated the percentage of time he should spend in each category. Now, instead of doing "more of it" — whatever "it" is — Paul dedicates 50% of his time to service and build-out meetings with clients, 35% of his time to new client meetings, 10% of his time to research, and 5% of his time to administrative work. This level of precision would irritate some people. But Paul craves this kind of clarity, because it helps him understand "what is expected" of him every day — the first, most critical element of engagement.

WHAT YOU DO BEST, EVERY DAY

As Paul's story illustrates, taking charge of your own engagement can be liberating. Becoming engaged starts with knowing your strengths and then assessing your engagement. Consider the elements of engagement. Do your opinions count? Are you making them known? If you are, are you bringing them up in a constructive manner? Do you have the materials and equipment you need? Have you asked for them? If you have asked and haven't received, do you know why? Do you have opportunities to learn and grow? Have you evaluated what skills and knowledge you're lacking and looked for ways to fill those gaps? And most importantly, have you talked to your manager?

All those things are in your power to achieve, but even the world's best boss can't provide them without your active participation. Getting your manager on board is a good first step toward boosting your engagement, but you'll also need to be receptive to what your manager has to say. You need to be open about what you need and be accountable for your emotional responses. The benefit will be a boost in your engagement — and your sales.

Try this exercise as a starting point. Look back at the 12 elements of engagement. Imagine that 11 of those elements are going to vanish off the page. You can only save one, and it's the one element that you feel has the biggest impact on your personal engagement. Which one would you save? Why that one? Now, go talk about that one element with your manager. You'll have taken the first step in managing your own engagement.

ENGAGEMENT IS GOOD FOR BUSINESS

Gallup has found that strengths development results in higher levels of employee engagement, and higher employee engagement is good for business. Compared to business units in the bottom 25%, the most engaged 25% of all the business units Gallup has studied have:

- 37% less absenteeism
- 25% less turnover in high-turnover organizations (such as sales)
- 49% less turnover in low-turnover organizations
- 27% less shrinkage
- 49% fewer safety incidents
- 60% fewer product defects
- 12% more engaged customers
- 18% higher productivity
- 16% greater profitability

This is how the numbers work in real life: Sony Europe takes employees' strengths so seriously that they've created "Super Teams," groups of volunteers who focus their talents on performance issues selected by the company. In 2004, according to *Strategic HR Review*, Sony implemented this strengths-based approach in Turkey. By 2005, sales had increased by 41%, the company was 20% ahead of budget, profit increased by 50%, and employee engagement improved by 10%.

STRENGTHS APPLIED: ENGAGING YOURSELF

Here are some ideas for engaging yourself using specific talent themes. Now think about your talents and strengths, and come up with some ideas for how you can increase your engagement using your own top five themes.

1. Example: Futuristic

   What will increase your engagement moving into the future? Learn about long-term plans that will energize you.

2. Example: Maximizer

   Look for ways to strengthen your engagement by finding the things that are working well and capitalizing on them even more.

3. Example: Strategic

   Make plans for improving your engagement. When things aren't going well, what are your back-up plans for reigniting your engagement?

4. Example: Relator

   Who gives you positive energy? Who can you turn to when you need to recharge your batteries? Make sure to consistently connect with these important individuals.

5. Example: Achiever

    Pay attention to how higher levels of achievement play into your engagement. Take stock of how you feel after reaching a new milestone or outpacing your past sales performance. Become aware of how accomplishments feed your engagement.

The Myth of Work/Life Balance

THIS CHAPTER'S KEY POINTS

- Work/life balance is a myth. Realizing that we can work toward a more integrated life, rather than a balanced life, is the first step toward building a stronger sense of wellbeing.

- There is no end date to integration — you won't ever "win." Integration is how you live your life every day. And it will never be perfect. But if it's too imperfect, ask for help.

- You cannot do it alone. You need to tell the important people in your life that you're working on integration, ask for their help, explain how they benefit, and get their buy-in.

- You have to think small. If you don't try to achieve "work versus family," but rather think in terms of lesser manageable chunks that make sense, you will be more successful.

- Integration takes time and effort. Understanding how your talents work for and against integration will help you develop them into strengths that you can use to gain a holistic perspective of yourself.

This is the challenge with a life in sales: the workday never ends. Here's the good thing: the workday never ends. People with a talent for sales often feel that their job is all-encompassing. They think about their customers while they read the paper, while they eat lunch, while they're on vacation, and while they're trying to get to sleep at night. Customers, and their needs and potential, are ever present.

We've just upped the ante with this book. As you learn more about your talents and how to apply them, as your productivity increases, as you get better at and more engaged with your job, you'll think more about work. You'll find new ways to reach and engage customers, to find advocates, and to create and sustain enduring relationships. You will create something that never ends — a job in sales — an even bigger part of your life.

However, there are other parts of your life. And if you're like many salespeople, you might not feel like you're giving them as much time, attention, and energy as you'd like. Your job may provide a constant hum in your mind. It might even be the most satisfying part of your life, and that's fine. But if the hum is drowning out other people, and they're bothered by it, it's not OK. Remember, if something you do gets in your way or gets in the way of others, it's a weakness. Over and over, we've heard about angry spouses, disappointed kids, regretted promotions (and demotions) — and always, always guilt. These are all real issues that shouldn't be taken lightly. Ultimately, what most salespeople are looking for is that mythical state called work/life balance.

We began this book by debunking some myths about sales. And now we'll argue against another commonly accepted myth — that you *can* balance work and life. The problem with this idea is the very word *balance*. Balance implies equality. The term suggests that one side of the equation equals the other side. In math, that's easy. In life, it isn't. It's an inherently flawed concept. Seeking balance puts people in a frenzied sprint, darting back and forth trying to keep the scales even and everyone happy, and this takes tremendous energy.

Then, when we think we have figured it out, life dumps something on one side of the scale and screws everything up — a big project at the office with major career implications, an elderly parent who suddenly needs extra attention and care, or a spouse who wants to start grad school. There's no such thing as balance, not in a world that changes so rapidly and unexpectedly.

REFRAMING YOUR APPROACH

Seeking balance is hard, and it forces you to compartmentalize — or put walls around the "work" you and the "home" you. That's not good for you, your job, or your life. Instead of seeking short-term balance, think about long-term integration. It might be impossible for you to compartmentalize your personal life and your job because your work as a salesperson is a big part of who you naturally are.

Or is it? We ask this question in all seriousness. There are several keys to integration, and one of them is being honest with yourself about how well you fit your role. If you feel like your life is completely disintegrated, you probably should be asking yourself if you're in the right job. One sales rep told us that he struggled with work/life balance for years, and he didn't understand why. He finally realized that the disconnection began when he was promoted to sales manager, and it was the wrong role for him. So he told his boss that he was quitting management and that he wanted a job in sales.

Being in the wrong job creates havoc. It forces people to work hard just to achieve mediocrity. They spend all their time trying to keep up with people who are a better fit for the role, and they never perform as well as they'd like. This is dispiriting, and this bad feeling follows people home. It affects their sense of pride and the quality time they spend in other areas of their lives.

If this describes you, your current role may not be the right one for you. But if only one or two aspects of your job bother you, think creatively about how to deal with them. One sales rep we interviewed did just that, but accidentally. Paperwork was his biggest battle. His wife could tolerate the long hours he spent at work, but she hated the long hours he spent doing paperwork at home. He did too — he would have rather been spending time with his family. They argued about it repeatedly. Then, after one argument too many, he snapped at his wife, "Fine. You do the paperwork!" He wasn't serious, just cranky. But her response changed everything. Matter-of-factly, she said, "Why don't I? I'm pretty good at that kind of thing. Why couldn't you pay me to do your paperwork?" They looked at each other like they had just discovered the cure for the common cold and realized they had found the solution. By creating a complementary partnership, this couple figured out a way to create more alignment in their lives. (For more on developing complementary partnerships, see the Appendix.)

Balance means equal. However, something can be equal to, but totally out of sync with, something else. On one side of the scale, you can have a ham sandwich and on the other side, some marbles. There's no correlation between those things other than the fact that they weigh the same. Now think about the most important things you're doing this week. What do they have in common? If you're trying to balance work and life, probably not much.

But when you think about integration rather than balance, the relationship is different. You're not trying to equalize everything; you're trying to bring different elements into alignment with one another. That might sound difficult, but it's an easier way to live.

THE FOUR RULES

There are four rules to integration:

1. *There is no end date to integration.* Integration isn't like a race with a start and a finish; there is no end point to integrating your life. It's how you live every day.

2. *You cannot do it alone.* You have to tell people — especially the most important people in your life — that you're working on integration. Ask for their help, explain how they benefit, and get their buy-in.

3. *You have to think small.* Pare the elements down to chunks that make sense: not "work versus family," but "appointment scheduling versus eating dinner before 10:00 p.m."

4. *Integration is never perfect.* If it's too imperfect, ask someone for assistance.

Martin, one of the people we interviewed, integrated an important element of his life using the four rules. Martin covers a large territory and drives from client to client. He found that as he planned his week, he would feel great about making all his calls and guilty about missing his daughter's softball games. Martin's integration answer finally came to him one day. It was his daughter's season opener, and he couldn't stand missing it. So he called a client and admitted that he wanted to reschedule a meeting so he could go to the game. The customer was more than willing to adjust the visit by a day or so to accommodate him.

While he watched the game, Martin formed a plan. The next day, he pulled out his client roster and put asterisks by his family-oriented customers (there were only three). He put circles by his most flexible customers. And he put Xs by the customers who would be dismayed to be asked such a thing. He called the customers with asterisks by their names, told them he was trying to make some of his daughter's softball games, and asked if they would mind rescheduling their meetings. He asked the ones with circles if they'd mind meeting on Mondays and Thursdays. And he accepted that the meetings with customers with Xs were unmovable.

In the end, Martin wound up driving an extra 75 miles a week to accommodate his daughter's softball schedule, but he began seeing a lot more games, and his daughter was touched that he made the effort. The family-oriented clients think he's a great dad, and the rest have no inkling of Martin's integration initiative.

A PROFOUND ISSUE

Most issues of work/life integration are basic time-and-place problems and can be solved relatively easily, as Martin's were. No one can be in two places at once, so you make compromises. But sometimes the issue of integration goes deeper than time and place. It goes to the heart of who you are.

Do you think Martin wasn't on his BlackBerry with clients during softball games? Of course he was. Do you think his mind didn't wander to the outfield during client presentations? Of course it did. He accepted that and considered it multitasking. In other words, once Martin gave himself permission to combine crucial elements of his life, he stopped feeling that dropping his strict work/life boundaries was weak or unprofessional.

Finally, Martin recognized that integration made him saner. He began using all of himself in everything he did and became more present in his own life. This made him better at whatever he was doing, because he wasn't reserving part of himself for something else. In the end, it worked because Martin used his talents to maintain the integration.

Martin used his Empathy talents to call clients and ask them to reschedule. He opened himself up to his clients and invited them to respond in kind. He used his Arranger talents to orchestrate schedules with his customers. After he started applying his talents to the problem of meetings versus softball, he became more skilled at using this approach to integrate other areas of his life. It became a habit. Essentially, integration became a psychological, rather than a time, issue. Martin trained himself to think of his life as a cohesive whole, with many things to do and enjoy, rather than a series of boxes to inhabit temporarily.

No, Martin didn't tell his boss he'd miss the sales retreat because his soul needed a fishing trip. And he knew better than to talk about his daughter to his clients who wouldn't care. But he stopped putting up boundaries between his work and the rest of his life and consciously worked to align them. It freed his mind — and a considerable amount of energy.

IT TAKES WORK

Integration isn't something that can be cobbled together over a weekend. Honing talents into strengths requires a long hard look at yourself. Once you discover your talents, you need to intentionally develop them. You need to put in time, energy, thought, and creativity. And by consciously developing talents and applying them, you'll gain a holistic perspective of yourself. Will this do wonderful things for your career? Yes. But this integrated outlook won't be confined to work. You'll find that you're applying the best of yourself to everything you do, including making time for things that are important to you and your family.

You will not, however, magically improve your work or your life just by reading this book — or any book. A strengths-based approach takes dedication and work. You must invest the time to sharpen your strengths. Don't just think about an interesting way to use your top five themes. Read, learn, and think about them — and then apply them.

Building strengths is a lifelong process. But like exercising and eating right, building strengths delivers results. When you put the ideas from this book into play, you'll see the difference in your relationships with your family, your coworkers, your customers, and your boss. You'll feel more engaged at work. You'll feel more connected at home. What's more, you will feel, quite simply, less fragmented and more complete.

We hope this chapter has helped you understand how integration can work in your life. We hope this book has given you ideas for long-term success in sales. In the end, we hope that all the elements of your life come together to help you achieve success not only as a salesperson, but also as a whole person. That is what the strengths-based approach is all about. It's about understanding and honoring the whole person. It's about recognizing that we aren't perfect and never will be. We can, however, be the best possible version of ourselves if we understand and tap into our talents and strengths — and the talents and strengths of others.

STRENGTHS APPLIED: THE MYTH OF WORK/LIFE BALANCE

Here are some ideas for integrating your life using specific talent themes. Now think about your talents and strengths, and come up with some ideas for how you can integrate your life more effectively using your own top five themes.

1. Example: Analytical

    Keep your top five themes with you. Jot them down on a piece of paper that you keep nearby. Read through them frequently, and analyze how you have been successfully applying them. Consider the dynamics between the themes. How are they complementing one another, and how could you use them even more?

2. Example: Includer

    Try to find ways to help others be a part of your strengths discovery process. Get them to take the Clifton StrengthsFinder assessment, and share your themes with one another in groups or teams. The more people you include in the process, the more you will have the opportunity to explore how the strengths approach is affecting your life.

3. Example: Consistency

As you work through decisions, make a list of pros and cons to help you understand all sides of the story. You may want to ask others to explain their point of view, especially when their opinion is contrary to what seems to be a fair outcome in your eyes. Be a resource for others by helping them understand how to ensure that the decisions being made are impartial and even-handed.

4. Example: Developer

Look for opportunities to help others — coworkers, friends, and family — grow and succeed through their strengths. As you help them apply their strengths and integrate their lives, you will make discoveries about yourself and grow as well. After all, you'll be applying your own strengths in the process.

5. Example: Belief

Know that what you are doing is incredibly meaningful. You are giving yourself a chance to be the best version of you possible. Because of this, you will have a positive and productive impact on the world around you. You will be more engaged, which means you will engage others. You will find more success, and you will be able to share that success with others. Stay on course with your strengths, and build a better world.

Talent Theme Definitions and Action Items

Talent themes, though they manifest themselves differently in everyone, guide us in quite predictable ways. For each of the 34 Clifton StrengthsFinder talent themes, we've provided a brief definition and some action items you can apply to your work in sales. The more you understand your talent themes, the better you can use them. And the more you use them, the better your sales performance will be.

ACHIEVER

People who are especially talented in the Achiever theme have a great deal of stamina and work hard. They take great satisfaction from being busy and productive.

> **ACTION:** Set your own goals and timelines. They are often larger and more aggressive than those you are assigned. This will help you feel more in charge of sales opportunities.

> **ACTION:** Take time to celebrate your successes, even momentarily, before moving on to the next item. Especially in long-term sales cycles, pay attention to small wins.

> **ACTION:** You are naturally equipped to work harder and longer than others. Be sure to schedule regular breaks to keep your battery charged so you can stay energized every day.

> **ACTION:** You might find sitting still in meetings difficult. Plan ahead, understand the meeting objectives, and help move individuals steadily through information. You will feel that your time is used more efficiently when you can manage the pace.

ACTIVATOR

People who are especially talented in the Activator theme can make things happen by turning thoughts into action. They are often impatient.

ACTION: Look for ways to be independent. Freedom and autonomy allow you to think about and act on sales opportunities without interference.

ACTION: Find secondary activities to keep you interested when you are in a holding pattern as part of a long-term sales cycle. Time when you have nothing to do is not good for you.

ACTION: Seek creative ways to keep your sales pipeline full. Proactively prospect and cold call to stay ahead of the game.

ACTION: Move quickly to identify solutions when your prospects or customers seem to be indecisive. This will rapidly build advocacy as people look to you for answers.

ADAPTABILITY

People who are especially talented in the Adaptability theme prefer to "go with the flow." They tend to be "now" people who take things as they come and discover the future one day at a time.

ACTION: Take on challenging sales situations that are in a state of flux. You are more likely to see possibilities when others might be stuck in what's tried and true.

ACTION: Calm those who are frustrated when the sales environment seems chaotic. When they see that you are relaxed and confident as you work to find solutions, they might be more inclined to find a peaceful resolution to a problem.

ACTION: Educate others when new circumstances arise. Barriers are commonplace in the sales process, and you seem to respond to these new events easily. Clarify what is happening and why.

ACTION: Adapt when you can; stand firm when you must. Your flexibility allows you to negotiate in a way that makes sense for the situation.

ANALYTICAL

People who are especially talented in the Analytical theme search for reasons and causes. They have the ability to think about all the factors that might affect a situation.

ACTION: Focus on customers with realistic potential as well as existing customers who can grow or spend more. Your attention to this information will help you identify sound prospects.

ACTION: Share what you know with your partners as it relates to sales growth. Helping your team understand where the greatest potential lies is likely to make prospecting and cold calling more effective for everyone involved.

ACTION: Create reports that show the buying patterns of your customers. This will help you understand those patterns and tie them to retention of the business. You'll also see potential for growth more clearly.

ACTION: Research sales information as it pertains to your customers. The numbers will help you assess short-term and long-term opportunities as you analyze their buying tendencies.

ARRANGER

People who are especially talented in the Arranger theme can organize, but they also have a flexibility that complements this ability. They like to figure out how all the pieces and resources can be arranged for maximum productivity.

ACTION: Pull together the needs, wants, and schedules of the various people involved in the sales process. This will ensure a smooth progression from beginning to end.

ACTION: Let customers see that your flexibility allows you to accommodate their requests. You build advocacy when you find ways to help and support them.

ACTION: You easily sort to the best solutions, so position yourself as the person who can make complicated sales situations feel less cumbersome.

ACTION: Because you are typically comfortable multitasking, you will benefit from having a number of customers who are at different stages in the sales process. Help your manager see how you easily manage a full pipeline.

BELIEF

People who are especially talented in the Belief theme have certain core values that are unchanging. Out of these values emerges a defined purpose for their life.

ACTION: You are genuine and motivated by more than just money. Let your customers see that you have underlying principles that define who you are, why you sell, and the value you can bring to them.

ACTION: Foster a values-based relationship with your customers. This will be the foundation for long-term partnerships; it will lay the groundwork for future retention and growth.

ACTION: Help team members and customers understand your beliefs about the products or processes you sell. For some, speaking to their hearts will cultivate a feeling of partnership that can lead to long-term commitments.

ACTION: Understand your customers' perspectives. You will find that negotiations are easier when you understand what is important to them and figure out how to sell to their beliefs.

COMMAND

People who are especially talented in the Command theme have presence. They can take control of a situation and make decisions.

ACTION: You are likely to be direct and outspoken. Moving quickly to the close may come naturally as you get to the heart of the matter. Be mindful that your natural presence can be intimidating to some. Take a moment to tailor your approach when necessary.

ACTION: Step up and break bottlenecks. You get customers moving, so use that decisive force to get them to say yes.

ACTION: Control discussions, address vital points on the agenda, and summarize key objectives as you assess opportunities, negotiate, and move people toward a decision. Prospects are likely to appreciate your to-the-point, make-it-happen style.

ACTION: You have a compelling presence, so ask for in-person meetings with customers, especially in your initial interactions. You are more likely to move face-to-face sales opportunities forward.

COMMUNICATION

People who are especially talented in the Communication theme generally find it easy to put their thoughts into words. They are good conversationalists and presenters.

> **ACTION:** Develop an effective catchphrase that drives the point of your sales approach home. You may find that prospecting is more productive when prospects remember your message.

> **ACTION:** Tell stories based on customer experiences. Prospects and customers alike may be more attentive when you tell stories that have relevance to their culture.

> **ACTION:** Be aware of what form of communication works best with each customer. Use that information to customize your message for your target audience.

> **ACTION:** You enjoy talking, so make sure your sales efforts are interactive rather than one-sided. As you assess your opportunities and look for solutions with customers, ask questions and listen.

COMPETITION

People who are especially talented in the Competition theme measure their progress against the performance of others. They strive to win first place and revel in contests.

ACTION: You want to know how you stack up against others, so consistently look at the numbers that make the most sense for your sales environment. Find ways to compare yourself to something or someone. Whether you compete against your own performance numbers or those of a colleague, you will be energized when you know how you are doing.

ACTION: When possible, go head-to-head with others. If direct competition is not feasible, identify the targets you want to overtake. It will keep you thinking about how close you are to winning.

ACTION: Identify what types of recognition are likely to energize you. Tell your manager what you need from him or her to stay excited about your achievements.

ACTION: Monitor your sales performance. If your manager does not routinely keep an eye on numbers, share your accomplishments to keep him or her in the loop and your eye on the prize.

CONNECTEDNESS

People who are especially talented in the Connectedness theme have faith in the links between all things. They believe there are few coincidences and that almost every event has a reason.

> **ACTION:** You seek to be a conduit, so become the link between your company and your customer. You naturally manage the flow between divergent groups with differing points of view.

> **ACTION:** You can see potential benefits to your customers. Explain those advantages, and link a problem with its solution. This will help prospects understand your course of action and the intended outcomes.

> **ACTION:** Paint a picture of why your partnership with the customer makes so much sense. Tie all the pieces and parts together to build bridges that become support systems in your customer group.

> **ACTION:** Because of the correlations you readily see between people and processes, you may notice sales growth opportunities that others do not. Link your products to the individuals or companies you are trying to close to help them see how your solutions fit into their broader company picture.

CONSISTENCY

People who are especially talented in the Consistency theme are keenly aware of the need to treat people the same. They try to treat everyone in the world with consistency by setting up clear rules and adhering to them.

ACTION: Stay committed to what you and your sales organization have promised. Customers will appreciate that you stay focused on the fair thing to do, even in difficult situations.

ACTION: Be the one to communicate bad news to customers. You understand the rationale behind decisions, and you can help others see why the decision was right and reasonable.

ACTION: You understand that at times, stronger personalities garner more attention and accolades. Steer praise to the person who has earned it — both inside the customer organization and within your own company. Others will appreciate your support, and you will develop advocates for the future.

ACTION: Find partners who can help you understand individual differences in customers. You can be the voice for evenhandedness while remaining aware that unique circumstances may dictate different solutions.

CONTEXT

People who are especially talented in the Context theme enjoy thinking about the past. They understand the present by researching its history.

ACTION: Think about what has worked in the past in terms of your sales success. Take what you know and find ways to use those best practices moving forward.

ACTION: Seek out people who have different sales experiences. Ask what has worked for them so that you don't keep reinventing the wheel.

ACTION: Study the histories of your prospects and customers. When you demonstrate a historical perspective as part of your sales approach, prospects are likely to appreciate the effort you made to become a valuable partner, and they will have a better understanding of the future you project.

DELIBERATIVE

People who are especially talented in the Deliberative theme are best described by the serious care they take in making decisions or choices. They anticipate the obstacles.

ACTION: You readily provide a great deal of detailed information, so make yourself ask the customer, "Should I explain more, or is that enough for your needs?" The sales process may move forward more quickly if you take cues from the customer.

ACTION: Before you step in front of your customers and prospects, thoroughly gather information pertaining to them. This will help you classify which prospects have potential and which customers can grow.

ACTION: Invest care and precision when planning your sales approach. With your homework completed, you are more likely to respond easily to objections and proceed with confidence.

ACTION: Take the time to understand individual styles, motivations, and personalities. Recognizing these differences up front could help move the sales process forward smoothly.

DEVELOPER

People who are especially talented in the Developer theme recognize and cultivate the potential in others. They spot the signs of each small improvement and derive satisfaction from these improvements.

ACTION: Find ways to help your customers look good in the eyes of their team members. When you set people up for success, you are likely to create advocates who support you as you move through the sales process.

ACTION: You typically see the best in people and situations, so be aware that you can over-invest in some sales environments. Take the time to logically weigh pros and cons as you investigate good sales opportunities.

ACTION: You are likely to enjoy interactive selling rather than a one-sided approach. Engage your audience whenever possible. You may find that you quickly develop camaraderie.

ACTION: You get a kick out of seeing other people excel. Get involved in post-sale training whenever possible. This will foster long-term relationships in the client's culture.

DISCIPLINE

People who are especially talented in the Discipline theme enjoy routine and structure. Their world is best described by the order they create.

ACTION: Whether you are involved in short-term or long-term sales cycles, you will want to establish and define objectives. Use your sense of structure to help maintain control as you move through the sales process.

ACTION: Institute a management system to stay aware of what is happening with each customer and prospect. Clients and prospects will see that you are dependable as you track commitments and deadlines.

ACTION: Tell your manager and partners that you prefer structure to surprise. This will keep your internal connections running smoothly as you work sequentially through the sales cycle.

EMPATHY

People who are especially talented in the Empathy theme can sense the feelings of other people by imagining themselves in others' lives or others' situations.

ACTION: Position yourself as a partner who supports your customers' issues and concerns. Identify what is important to them, and then sell to their needs.

ACTION: You will pick up on discomfort, confusion, and frustration from prospects during the sales process. Adjust accordingly as you keep the sale on track.

ACTION: You easily tap into customers' and prospects' thoughts. Look for opportunities to speak a language that makes sense to them. They are likely to feel that you're uniquely capable of understanding what they need and how you can help.

ACTION: There might be times when you feel that objections have been left unsaid. Ask questions that demonstrate to others that you understand their concerns and want to respond to them. This will foster trust both in the moment and over the long haul.

FOCUS

People who are especially talented in the Focus theme can take a direction, follow through, and make the corrections necessary to stay on track. They prioritize, then act.

ACTION: Put a quarterly or yearly plan into place that defines short-term and long-term goals. Then surround that plan with benchmarks that help you make those targets become reality.

ACTION: Think ahead three to five years, and attach quantifiable sales objectives to the future. When you clarify your definition of sales success and how you want to get it, you are likely to stay the course and make it happen.

ACTION: Share short-term and long-term goals with your manager and other work partners. With a tangible game plan in place, you can ask your manager to support your success.

ACTION: Focus on learning from the best in your environment. Knowing what you do well and incorporating it with the success model of other top performers keeps you on track as you assess long-term opportunities.

FUTURISTIC

People who are especially talented in the Futuristic theme are inspired by the future and what could be. They inspire others with their visions of the future.

ACTION: Ask your customers intelligent questions about their future. Whether they are thinking about stock price, growth in sales dollars, or increase in number of clients served, they will appreciate your connection to their future state.

ACTION: Help prospects and customers visualize where your products or services can take them. Explain possibilities, and link that information to retention, growth, market penetration, or other future plans. When you discuss future options, be sure to stay grounded in the present. Customers may be more willing to buy when they see how your far-reaching ideas take root in their world today.

ACTION: Involve yourself whenever possible in the product or solution design stage with customers. You can push them beyond the here and now toward exploring opportunities and solutions for the long term.

ACTION: Understand your market. When you show aptitude and knowledge in the environment where you sell, you will more readily help prospects tap into what could be as they look toward the future.

HARMONY

People who are especially talented in the Harmony theme look for consensus. They don't enjoy conflict; rather, they seek areas of agreement.

ACTION: Look for common ground as part of your sales process. You have an agreeable sales approach that tends to foster a sense of camaraderie and partnership early on.

ACTION: Without a doubt, there will be periods of apprehension as you move prospects toward the close, regardless of what product you sell. Use your ability to listen, understand their anxiety, and lend a reassuring perspective to allay their discomfort.

ACTION: You are often considered to be the problem solver. Because you understand boundaries, others will look to you to find a point of connection. Help move people closer to resolving obstacles and closing the deal.

ACTION: Be the go-to person when others need to be convinced that the decisions they make are correct. You establish trust by finding common ground as you work to build consensus among all the parties involved.

IDEATION

People who are especially talented in the Ideation theme are fascinated by ideas. They are able to find connections between seemingly disparate phenomena.

ACTION: Think about new and different ways of achieving results with prospects and customers. They will quickly see how creative and resourceful your ideas are.

ACTION: Be a brainstorming partner with your fellow salespeople. You will build a solid constituency inside your organization as others hear your ideas for prospecting and closing business. These interactions will also stimulate your own thoughts on market penetration and growth.

ACTION: Ask your customers and prospects thought-provoking questions. You'll inspire possibility thinking within your customer base. This will give you time in front of others as well as the opportunity for future business.

ACTION: Figure out what activates your good ideas. When you are aware of what stimulates creative ideas and sound solutions, you can use that trigger mechanism to outline selling strategies for new as well as loyal customers.

INCLUDER

People who are especially talented in the Includer theme are accepting of others. They show awareness of those who feel left out, and make an effort to include them.

ACTION: You're uniquely capable of making everyone — gatekeepers, requisition managers, buyers, decision makers — feel important as part of the sales cycle. Use this talent to build advocacy quickly.

ACTION: Spend time with as many of your connections in the customer's environment as possible. More is better as you look for inroads into organizations.

ACTION: Appreciate that prospects and customers as well as your internal customer support team can benefit from being included in the sales process. Let them know the positive impact they create.

ACTION: Because you naturally include others, you are likely to find ways to gather information from many people as you work to understand the goals and objectives of your prospects. Invite them in, ask questions, and answer concerns throughout the sales cycle.

INDIVIDUALIZATION

People who are especially talented in the Individualization theme are intrigued with the unique qualities of each person. They have a gift for figuring out how people who are different can work together productively.

ACTION: Because you easily appreciate the unique qualities of each customer and prospect, find opportunities to customize strategies and solutions that suit each person and organization.

ACTION: Listen to your Individualization talents during interactions with customers and prospects. You can perceive what others are thinking, and you pick up on signals that others miss.

ACTION: Your insights will help you tap into unexpressed needs and concerns. Make this awareness work for you as you ask smart questions, understand fears, and come up with sound solutions.

ACTION: Match products and solutions to the needs of your customers. They will sense that you understand them when you can easily help them see how your products link to their requirements.

INPUT

People who are especially talented in the Input theme have a craving to know more. Often they like to collect and archive all kinds of information.

ACTION: Learn and speak your customers' language. This will demonstrate to them that you are aware of who they are and what they need.

ACTION: Become an expert in your company. As you gather sound information and share what you know about customers and products, others will begin to see you as an advisor. This will position you well to build strong internal partnerships.

ACTION: Gather comprehensive and helpful client information early in the sales process. When you speak knowledgeably about their culture, prospects will believe that you are invested in them and that you can offer valuable insights.

ACTION: Immerse yourself in your customers' needs. Study, learn, and understand their short-term and long-term goals. This will be valuable as you work through various sales opportunities.

INTELLECTION

People who are especially talented in the Intellection theme are characterized by their intellectual activity. They are introspective and appreciate intellectual discussions.

> **ACTION:** Take time each day to just think. It is important for you to collect and organize your thoughts as you contemplate sales strategies. Taking this valuable thinking time will help you feel more confident as you move forward in the sales process.

> **ACTION:** Generate hypotheses as you move through the strategy phase of the sales process. You have the ability to help prospects think through solutions and implementation plans.

> **ACTION:** Work with others on your sales team as you figure out how to maneuver around hurdles. Brainstorming can help unlock possibilities as you organize thoughts and strategies.

> **ACTION:** Collaborate with various teams in your customer organizations. You are energized by the thinking process, and group interaction is a sound way of sharing ideas, sorting through possibilities, and inspiring new points of view. Your client group will likely appreciate being included in these brainstorming sessions as you assess opportunities and solutions together.

LEARNER

People who are especially talented in the Learner theme have a great desire to learn and want to continuously improve. In particular, the process of learning, rather than the outcome, excites them.

ACTION: Figure out how you learn best. If you can understand and use your learning system efficiently, you will gain customer and prospect knowledge and quickly become productive. Study what has made you successful in the past. Concentrating on how you moved a former prospect to a successful close will allow you to recreate that strategy in the future.

ACTION: Thoroughly research your prospects before cold calls. You are at your best when you know your stuff, and this knowledge will impress decision makers and help set the stage for an efficient negotiation phase.

ACTION: Learn alongside your prospects and customers. Ask smart questions. When they see that you willingly invest time to learn about who they are and what they need, you may gain an edge over other salespeople.

ACTION: Look for complicated sales roles that push you to know more. The challenge is in the knowing, and you typically find complex selling situations stimulating.

MAXIMIZER

People who are especially talented in the Maximizer theme focus on strengths as a way to stimulate personal and group excellence. They seek to transform something strong into something superb.

> **ACTION:** You will be most energized when you can turn a potential customer into a long-lasting customer. Keep your focus where you have the greatest opportunity to develop long-term relationships and to reach top levels of success.

> **ACTION:** Identify the aspects of your product or service that will be most beneficial to your prospects. You will naturally focus on what is relevant to your customers, so make sure that what you are offering is the best possible solution.

> **ACTION:** You have a good sense of who has potential as you explore top prospects. Figure out who is likely to benefit the most from your products and services, and determine which decision makers you should give the most attention.

> **ACTION:** Always think about how you can make things a little better or move them along a little faster. You want to improve and excel, so look for ways to maximize your efforts so that you can add value for your customers and prospects.

POSITIVITY

People who are especially talented in the Positivity theme have an enthusiasm that is contagious. They are upbeat and can get others excited about what they are going to do.

ACTION: You naturally inspire optimism, so begin each sale by asking questions about the good things that are happening in the prospect's organization. When appropriate, don't hesitate to lighten the environment with humor. Using wit in the sales process can be a good icebreaker and can foster strong partnerships.

ACTION: Your ability to inspire good feelings can open many doors. Recognize your customers as well as internal partners by highlighting what they do well. You will develop a valuable network of advocates as others appreciate your upbeat attitude.

ACTION: Tie your strong feelings of positivity to reality. Acknowledge challenging situations, but communicate the reasons for your optimism. Help others realize that difficulties do concern you, but there is good reason to remain optimistic.

ACTION: Build momentum by sharing your enthusiasm at various stages in the selling cycle. Customers can feel points of pain sometimes, and having the ability to put a positive note into the conversation can ease the tension at crucial times.

RELATOR

People who are especially talented in the Relator theme enjoy close relationships with others. They find deep satisfaction in working hard with friends to achieve a goal.

ACTION: You are at your best when you can cultivate and grow relationships with customers over the long term. Look for selling situations that allow you to sustain partnerships over time.

ACTION: Get to know your customers, understand their values, and pay attention to their goals. You naturally develop meaningful relationships, so find ways to foster that value in your sales interactions.

ACTION: You naturally connect with your customers not only as business associates but also as people. Pay attention to those who welcome personal partnerships, and work to build those relationships.

ACTION: Use the engaging aspects of your personality to put yourself out there. Others will see that you genuinely care, and you are likely to develop long-lasting connections that help build retention and growth with client organizations.

RESPONSIBILITY

People who are especially talented in the Responsibility theme take psychological ownership of what they say they will do. They are committed to stable values such as honesty and loyalty.

> **ACTION:** You want to be responsible for everything that happens with your customers and prospects. Look for consultative selling situations that allow you to be closely involved with all aspects of the sales cycle.

> **ACTION:** You need to do what you have committed to do. Pay attention to your customer load, and allow yourself to focus where you can most effectively and efficiently spend your time.

> **ACTION:** Because you are committed to quality and service, take on accounts and product lines that call for post-sale follow-through. You will embrace the feeling of following up and following through.

> **ACTION:** People will easily see and value your dependability. Draw on the trust you have established with your satisfied customers by asking for referrals.

RESTORATIVE

People who are especially talented in the Restorative theme are adept at dealing with problems. They are good at figuring out what is wrong and resolving it.

ACTION: You're most energized when you can figure out an obstacle and overcome it. Consider taking on big challenges that give you the opportunity and reward of turning things around.

ACTION: You have a natural foresight for potential trouble. So tackle not only existing problems, but also anticipate and prevent difficulties before they occur.

ACTION: Because you naturally want to find the reasons why something did not work, routinely review your sales process. Identify why you didn't win a certain sale or grow a particular opportunity with a customer. Thinking about the "why nots" should give you valuable insights.

ACTION: You have a natural awareness of challenges and solutions, so consciously apply your Restorative talents when you are cold calling. This will give you a head start as you assess opportunities and identify solutions before others do.

SELF-ASSURANCE

People who are especially talented in the Self-Assurance theme feel confident in their ability to manage their own lives. They possess an inner compass that gives them confidence that their decisions are right.

> **ACTION:** Rarely in doubt, you will find it advantageous to verify that you are on the most productive and successful sales path by bouncing ideas and strategies off your sales manager or others you trust. Let those you have confidence in be your barometer as you move through the sales process.

> **ACTION:** You exude confidence, so take the lead when introducing a new product, trying a new sales approach, or breaking into a new market.

> **ACTION:** You tend to inspire trust, so state your claims with authority and conviction. Be sure to back up your certainty with facts. Factual information is likely to get people on board quickly.

> **ACTION:** Review your customized approaches and the decisions you make on the fly during your sales process. This informal study will help ensure that your confidence is in line with your competence.

SIGNIFICANCE

People who are especially talented in the Significance theme want to be very important in the eyes of others. They are independent and want to be recognized.

ACTION: Strive to provide above-and-beyond service to each customer. You want others to see you as an important contributor to their success.

ACTION: Select sales opportunities that are tied to significant challenges and goals. You get satisfaction when you can achieve success and when others see the magnitude of the work you have accomplished. You will appreciate the affirmation that comes from a job done well.

ACTION: Share your goals with your manager or other important members of your team. Once you have committed out loud to your objectives, you will be determined to achieve them.

ACTION: Let your sales manager know that you appreciate praise, and communicate how you would like to be recognized. External accolades will energize you and push you to do more.

STRATEGIC

People who are especially talented in the Strategic theme create alternative ways to proceed. Faced with any given scenario, they can quickly spot the relevant patterns and issues.

ACTION: Consider alternatives as you explore the potential of your sales partnerships and the greatest opportunities for growth. This helps you understand your return on time invested as you cold call and prospect.

ACTION: Use your "what if" thinking to generate an extensive list of potential customers. This allows you to keep your pipeline full of new prospects.

ACTION: Cut to the chase quickly and logically. Keep your sales presentation thorough yet to the point, thus maximizing your time discussing solutions that make sense.

ACTION: Anticipate roadblocks and obstacles that might arise throughout the sales process. Evaluate the deals you are working on for possible hold-ups or glitches. Because you can foresee issues before they arise, this anticipation should keep the process moving toward a successful close.

WOO

People who are especially talented in the Woo theme love the challenge of meeting new people and winning them over. They derive satisfaction from breaking the ice and making a connection with another person.

ACTION: Find the right words to explain that networking is part of your style and that your need to sway people to your way of thinking is sincere. When others realize that you are genuine, it may be easier for you to pull them into a conversation.

ACTION: Make the most of your Woo talents by establishing as many connections as possible. Put the details of who you know and what you know about them into a usable format. When you can call archived information to mind, you will easily renew valuable connections. Check in at least once a month to keep those relationships alive and your network growing.

ACTION: In your sales relationships, intentionally move beyond the meet and greet as you get people to like you. Capitalize on your ability to win people over as you look for signals of buyer warmth.

ACTION: Your friendly demeanor draws people in. Use your outgoing nature to become a better negotiator. It allows everyone to leave the table with a win-win feeling.

Appendix:
Seven Ways to Sharpen Strengths and Manage Weaknesses

Learning how to maximize your strengths and minimize the time you spend managing weaknesses takes practice, effort, and creativity. Here are seven strategies to help you apply your efforts more effectively and overcome some challenges you might face.

1. Create open communication and transparency

In most organizations, people hide their weaknesses. But we think it's better to admit them and recognize how they may be holding you back or hindering others. Talk with your manager about where you're having trouble and why. More importantly, don't ever be embarrassed about what makes you great.

"I like to win," said Kelly Matthews, who is the account manager for an important account at Mars Snackfood. One of her top five themes is Competition. "I can spend time just going through the motions, or I can see what type of challenges are out there and go after [them]. I think that keeps the job fun. I think that's what makes life fun. You know, *winning*." Kelly's Competition talents take a lead role in her approach to sales, but two of her other top themes, Focus and Achiever, are what drive her to remain consistently productive and intent on her goals. She's also clearly focusing on her strengths, not obsessing over her weaknesses.

2. Intentionally use your strengths

At a large financial services firm, we conducted a meeting with one of the sales teams to discuss an upcoming strengths coaching session. The group was having a good time and was incredibly enthused. The meeting was more like a party than a business discussion. Then the sales vice president, whose top theme was Command, said, "We've all discussed our strengths. What about weaknesses? What's my biggest weakness?"

The room went silent. Everyone stared at the table. Finally, one account executive meekly looked up and said, "Well, when we have sales meetings, you kind of tend to, you know, do all the talking."

Another person, building on the comment from the first, muttered, "So sometimes we don't get the chance to tell you things."

A third offered, "Which means you don't always get all the information you need."

Then someone in the back whispered, "And we're all afraid to interrupt you."

This hit the V.P. hard, but he recognized the opportunity. After the meeting, he had his assistant type up his top five themes. He sent a copy to everyone on his team and called another meeting for a week later. He said, "These are my strengths. Tell me how to use them to make us better."

So his team showed him how his top talent themes, one by one, would be better served if he stopped taking over meetings. One of his top five themes is Competition. They told him that if he quit dominating discussions, they would sell — and thus win — more. Another one of his top five themes is Input. They told him that if he held his tongue a bit more in meetings, he'd learn more. Futuristic is also in his top five, and they told him that if he listened more, he'd get a clearer picture of what's on the horizon.

He wrote down all these suggestions on a list with his top five themes. He keeps the list by his phone, and he doesn't attend a meeting without thinking about some questions to ask before getting to his own agenda. Now every time he gathers his staff for a sales meeting, he's reminded of what happens when he uses his strengths intentionally — and stops taking over meetings.

3. Find support systems

A support system helps you with what you don't do well or gives you reinforcement when you need it. Support systems can be technological, such as programming a spreadsheet with macros that do the math on sales reports or reminder e-mails that you send to yourself. You can also establish a support system by developing new habits. For example, those who don't lead with Woo might find it challenging to make initial contacts or small talk with strangers. If Woo isn't one of your top talents, make a list of five small-talk topics and read it before you walk into a stranger's office.

Support systems can also be other people. Many of us would never remember a birthday if our spouses didn't remind us. "Over my 15 years, I created what I call my support network: my fellow reps, mentors, managers, corporate people whom I can call and kind of get talked off the ledge every once in a while," said Ron Barczak from Stryker. "People I can call and say OK, I need to vent for 10 minutes about something. Can I just vent to you? Because I cannot vent to my customers."

4. Build complementary partnerships

You build a complementary partnership by teaming up with someone who is strong in an area where you are weak. One of the best ways to create such a partnership is by offering your talents in exchange for someone else's. This works like a support system, but the difference is that you offer something up as well.

For instance, Communication isn't one of Carter's top talents, and he tends to move so quickly through the sales call that he misses opportunities to explain details or ask for feedback. But Ideation is one of his top five themes. Carter should look for someone with strong Communication talents to be his rehearsal audience. That person can help him think about what he needs to say, what questions he needs to ask, and when he needs to pause and listen. In return, Carter can offer to come up with ideas for solutions for his partner's clients.

Complementary partnering might help with a weakness that is extremely common in many sales forces: dealing with paperwork. Because so few sales reps enjoy paperwork, they may have trouble finding a partner for this on the sales team. Many account executives hire paperwork assistants on their own dime. This is a good tactic for freeing up more time and energy for activities that can drive sales rather than spending an enormous amount of time doing something badly.

If you can't find a partner, ask your boss for help. "I had a manager who would always say to me when things would get overwhelming, 'I'll cover the paperwork. I'll cover the organizational stuff. Go see your customers.' He knew that's where I would get my energy from," said John Wells from

Interface, whose top themes include Woo. "We all have to do things that we aren't the strongest in, but those are the things that zap your energy. A great manager's going to figure out, even around some seemingly rigid rules, how to do that for that person. And then that person's going to go over the mountain for his manager." So don't overlook the possibility that your boss can be a complementary partner too.

5. Get the right education

As we've noted, sales reps need training — the *right* kind of training. And that training doesn't rely on a rigid formula, program, or plan. The right training or development program is issue-based and specific. If you need better product knowledge, then this is a training issue. It's also a good idea to consider why the initial training program might not have done the trick. The right training accommodates individual strengths and learning styles. Those with Input might not mind reading a 400-page product manual, whereas strong Activators can be impatient to see the product in the field.

Jenny Craig has a training program that's designed to meet the needs of people who learn in different ways. "Our training program is all kinds of things," said TC Crafts from Jenny Craig. "It's information and dialogue and different scenarios that you can practice and believe in."

It's also important to note that *training* and *development* are not synonymous. Training is the opportunity to enhance your level of skills and/or knowledge. Marcy, a sales manager for a company that sells windows directly to consumers, went through a training program that concentrated on specifications. This program helped Marcy learn about the company's products, but it didn't help her learn how to use her talents to sell more effectively. This is where development comes in. Once she learned how to apply her talents to her role, she quickly hit her stride. If you can spot the difference between training deficiencies and development deficiencies, you're more likely to apply the correct solution to the problem.

6. Manage unpleasant tasks by focusing on the outcomes

In sales, there are some things you just have to do: sales reports, expense sheets, meeting logs. And if you're like most reps, you hate doing them. So agree with your manager on the activities that are not negotiable — the stuff you must do to keep your job. Negotiate a standard, a bare minimum, and get it done. More importantly, focus on the outcomes of those activities, not the steps.

For instance, a newspaper advertising rep we know despised figuring up her commissions every month. To do it, she had to pore over the paper, cut out all the ads she sold, measure them, figure the price, then look up whatever discount she'd given the buyer and subtract it to find the price. Once that was done, she had to do some complicated math to figure out her sales for the month, then more math to determine her cut. She couldn't find a complementary partner anywhere — all the ad reps hated figuring their commissions too.

Then she had a brainstorm. Instead of showing the math every month in one big spreadsheet, she asked her sales manager if she could submit her commissions on an ad-by-ad basis over the course of the month, then enter the results on a small spreadsheet. Her sales manager agreed, but on one condition: If her math was off, she'd have to go back to the original method. "I started noting the price of everything I sold as I sold it, right in my BlackBerry," she said. "It was a hard habit to get into, because I don't like record keeping. I'd prefer to sell and move on."

Though she didn't like keeping track that way, it did resolve half the trouble of figuring commissions at the end of the month. Her manager double checked the figures and found them to be more accurate than the sloppy math she'd cranked out under duress all those years. "Then, instead of putting [my commissions] off until the last minute and staying at the office until midnight the day my commission report was due, I started thinking of the ads in terms of stuff I wanted to buy. A 2x2 ad is a tank of gas," she said. "A 2x5 equals a pair of shoes. A full-page color ad is a house payment. I went through the paper looking for my potential purchases, measured ad by ad. I made a game out of it, and that made it more real and relevant."

Remember, all the things you don't like doing are only a small part of the job. That ad rep spent only five hours a month out of 200 figuring out her commission the old way. One of our clients said, "I loathe filling out reports, but it's only 5% of my day. When it hits 30%, I'll quit." That's true for you too. First, try to negotiate the things you hate doing down to a tolerable level. If you can't, here's the perfect opportunity for you to seek out support systems and complementary partnerships, even it if may mean pooling your resources and hiring for them.

7. Adjust or change roles

As a successful sales veteran, Geoff Nyheim from Microsoft Online Services — whose top five themes are Maximizer, Relator, Strategic, Achiever, and Input — realized over time that he's probably a better farmer than a hunter. "I have enough skins from successful hunts on my wall to add credibility. I've made my [sales] number 22 out of 24 years, and that didn't happen just because I was nice to people. But basically, I'm better at farming." So he has shifted to doing more of what he does best: creating and maintaining long-term relationships. He'd be much less successful at churn-and-burn selling, and he knows it.

Some situations, however, require more drastic changes. For instance, if you use only two of your top five themes at work, you might do better in another role. In the meantime, use your other strengths any way you can. Maximize your softball team. Focus on your piano playing. Solve the problem of your library's budget shortfall. Work is much more engaging, exciting, and rewarding when you use all your talents, but if you don't have that option right now, make sure you use them somewhere. You'll be amazed at how fulfilling it can be — and a little of that fulfillment will spill over into your job.

Acknowledgements

First, we would like to thank Gallup's clients. Every day, they provide us with wonderful, real-world environments in which we see talents come to life.

Ensuring that we earn the right to partner with our customers are our smart and talented Gallup colleagues, who are everything we could want as best friends at work. Rachel Penrod and Shawna Hubbard-Thomas have kept us on track every day. Tom Rath, Jan Miller, Joe Streur, Emily Meyer, Nikki Blacksmith, Jessica Tyler, Jim Asplund, Jim Harter, John Fleming, Bill Diggins, Diane Obrist-Lynam, Therese Nisbet, Jeannie Ruhlman, Cheryl Siegman, Anne Harbison, Jacque Merritt, Barry Conchie, Dana Baugh, Vandana Allman, Dan Kingkade, and Heather Wright have devoted their careers to studying excellence and helping people flourish. We thank you for the insights, wisdom, and stories.

We would also like to thank those internal partners who helped us to learn from their best clients — Kelly Aylward, Leslie Rowlands, John Wood, Steve Dosier, Jane Hart, Kevin Christoffersen, Ken Shearer, Randy Beck, Keith Roberts, Daniel Porcelli, Bill Reid, and Rolly Keenan — as well as those who work on development programs in the area of sales: Steven Beck, Dean Jones, Jamie Librot, Matt Mosser, Shari Theer, Joy Plemmons, Tonya Fredstrom, and Scot Caldwell.

We need to add a special thanks to Jim Clifton, Jane Miller, Jim Krieger, Connie Rath, and other Gallup leaders who give us the amazing opportunity to do our work with clients. We would be remiss without mentioning our world-class editor Geoff Brewer and business book gurus Larry Emond and Piotrek Juszkiewicz. Kelly Henry applied her customary perfectionism to both content editing and copy editing this book. And kudos to the very talented Samantha Allemang for her elegant design.

Very special recognition and praise go to Barb Sanford for her extraordinary attention to accuracy and quality. She edited drafts of this book while directing a thorough review of our concepts. Therese Nisbet, Jeannie Ruhlman, and Jan Miller devoted many hours to ensuring that our strengths concepts were as sharp and up to date as possible. Randy Beck offered superb insights into how the book could best be structured, and Kevin McConville and Ed O'Boyle provided tremendously helpful feedback as well.

Finally, this book would never have taken shape without Jennifer Robison. She was extraordinarily creative in helping us put down these words coherently and compellingly. Through the pregnancy and birth of her third child, Jennifer remained diligent in keeping after its mercurial and often missing authors. And, as she has done so many times in our *Gallup Management Journal*, she proved exceptionally adept at helping bring our research to life.

ABOUT THE AUTHORS

Tony Rutigliano is a Senior Practice Expert at Gallup, where he has worked for 16 years. He was also Vice President/Chief Learning Officer for ADP, where he oversaw initiatives and programs aimed at improving the organization's learning, leadership development, succession planning, performance management, and talent assessment capabilities. In addition, Rutigliano led many of the sales training and sales manager development efforts for ADP's force of more than 5,000 reps. Rutigliano coauthored *Discover Your Sales Strengths* (Warner Books, 2003), which is based on Gallup's work with more than 170 sales organizations. Before joining Gallup, Rutigliano was publisher and editor-in-chief of *Sales & Marketing Management* magazine. He lives in Randolph, New Jersey, with his wife, Karen Burns.

Brian J. Brim, Ed.D., is a Senior Practice Expert at Gallup. For more than 21 years, he has worked as a consultant, speaker, and advisor to some of the world's leading organizations. Brim is an executive coach to top leaders and plays a major role in creating and launching consulting offerings tied to employee selection, performance management, employee development, team dynamics, employee engagement, customer engagement, and succession planning. Brim regularly contributes articles to the *Gallup Management Journal,* and two of his articles were included in *The Best of the Gallup Management Journal 2001-2007.* He lives in Omaha, Nebraska, with his wife, Kimberly, and their two daughters, Chloe and Jerri.

Gallup Press exists to educate and inform the people who govern, manage, teach, and lead the world's six billion citizens. Each book meets Gallup's requirements of integrity, trust, and independence and is based on Gallup-approved science and research.